Baking, Making and Sharing

by
SUSAN OVER

By the same author:
Cakes, Bakes, Puddings and Prayers

Published by
The Leprosy Mission International
80 Windmill Road, Brentford
Middlesex TW8 0QH, United Kingdom

Edited and distributed by TLM Trading Limited (for address see page 72)
www.tlmtrading.com

Bible verses from the NIV (NEW INTERNATIONAL VERSION),
used by permission of the International Bible Society.
Bible verses from The Message by Eugene Petersen, published by Nav Press,
used with permission.

First Published 2007
© Susan Over

Design by Creative Plus Publishing Ltd,
2nd Floor, 151 High Street, Billericay, Essex, CM12 9AB
www.creative-plus.co.uk

Printed and bound in China
Phoenix Offset

A catalogue record for this book is available from the British Library.
ISBN 978-0-902731-67-7

Introduction

Isn't it lovely to give a gift that you think will be just right for someone and hear their words of pleasure? What a disappointment when the opposite happens and you can tell by the way the gift is quickly discarded that you didn't quite hit the mark!

I knew I hadn't quite got it right when I gave a newborn baby knitted bootees in the middle of summer – but they were so cute! His brother did rather better with a teddy bear sun-catcher personalised with his name, and that was the point – to make the older child feel included.

Whenever we give something away that we have personally created, we give a little bit of ourselves away with it. And the person receiving it knows how much they are valued because we have made an effort. Everything in this book can be made as a gift and they are all just starting points for you to develop to suit the people you know.

We don't know why God chose such a costly way of offering us eternal life. He sent his only, dearly loved son – part of *himself* – to die such a terrible death in our place. This will always be the greatest gift of all.

As you browse through the gifts and goodies and choose something to make for a special friend, remember that every one of us is more special to God than we can ever imagine. And all the good gifts he gives us are to equip us to spread his love to others as we journey towards eternity.

Susan Over, June 2007

Dedication

For Sophie and Katherine, our granddaughters,
who inspire and encourage me.

Acknowledgements

Photography by Tim Sandall.
All the recipes were tried, tested and baked for photography by Wendy Dyer,
Honor Harris, Susan Over, Judith Merrell and Katherine Turner.
Thanks team, for all your time and effort to make things just right.
Special thanks to Judith for the use of her kitchen for the photo shoot.

Personal Thoughts

Honor: The lollipop cookies were great fun to make and to give! The joy on people's faces as they munched them was a reward in itself. They'd be super for a birthday party!

Tim: The very cheesy *Nuggets of Gold* were great. We nearly ran out of them at the photo shoot because I couldn't stop eating them! We only just had enough left for the picture.

Wendy: It's good to make personal gifts for friends and this book makes it easier to do so. I enjoyed making the *Coffee Time Cookies* – they're an ideal gift when you're invited out to coffee.

Katherine: I am incredibly proud of my mum for what she has achieved with her first book *Cakes, Bakes, Puddings and Prayers*. I use it constantly and am looking forward to doing the same with this one. The *Ginger Fruit Jubilees* are really moreish; I'll be making them often.

Judith: The *Epiphany Cake* is quite delicious. I'll certainly make this again and again and not just at Christmas!

Susan: Just be creative with these ideas – and let me know how you get on!

Contents

Loving Truffles

Once you've tried these, you will forget anything you can buy on the High Street! Perfect for Valentine's Day, they make a lovely gift for someone special at any time of year. Present them in a heart-shaped box or basket for an added touch of class.

Truffles will keep for a week or more in the fridge – if they get the chance!
If a white hue develops on the chocolate, simply sprinkle with a little icing sugar before serving.

The ganache can also be made with milk chocolate or a mix of milk and plain according to taste. You could also add dried fruit, nuts or stem ginger.
Try a different spirit or liqueur such as rum or Grand Marnier. Add a little Tia Maria for a particularly delicious truffle.

Ingredients

For ganache filling:
350g (12oz) good plain chocolate
6 tablespoons double cream
4 tablespoons brandy

For coating:
Plain, milk or white chocolate, melted

Method

1 Roughly chop the chocolate for the ganache.
2 In a medium saucepan bring the cream to the boil. Remove from heat and stir in chocolate until completely melted.
3 Blend in brandy until all is absorbed.
4 Turn into a shallow container lined with cling-wrap and chill in the fridge for at least an hour.
5 When mixture is firm, turn onto surface dusted with icing sugar and roll into log shape. Cut off even pieces and roll into balls. (Rinse hands in cold water and dry between batches so that they don't become too sticky.)
6 Dip each truffle in melted chocolate and leave to set on baking parchment or grease-proof paper.
7 Once set, place each truffle in a paper sweet case.
Makes approximately 14–16 truffles.

> If I speak in the tongues of men and of angels, but have not love,
> I am only a resounding gong or a clanging cymbal.
> 1 Corinthians 13:1 (NIV)

No-one is quite sure how St Valentine's Day originated. Some say that the original saint was a Roman who was martyred on 14 February AD269 for refusing to give up Christianity. Legend has it that he left a farewell note signed *From Your Valentine* for his jailer's daughter who had befriended him.

It doesn't really matter as any excuse for sending loving messages to each other is alright by me! I remember a bumper year for Valentine cards when I received eight and thought I was extremely popular – until I found they had all been sent by the same person for a joke. Hmm...

In the Middle Ages, young men and women drew names from a bowl to see who their Valentine would be and they would then wear the name on their sleeves for a week. Wearing your heart on your sleeve means you are not afraid to show other people how you are feeling. A couple of my friends have a real ministry in encouraging me with a card or a letter in the post when I'm feeling the pressures of life and this helps me to know I'm loved.

There are different kinds of love – it's not all about eyes meeting across a crowded room! Sometimes love is an act of will and we have to reach out to someone towards whom we don't feel a natural affinity. Jesus was the master of this and often seemed to prefer the company of the disadvantaged in his society. The famous passage from the letter to the Corinthians on love, often used at weddings, is written in the context of using our spiritual gifts for the benefit of each other. Paul makes the point that whatever other gifts we are exercising, they are useless unless we practise real love, even in the most difficult circumstances.

So, if you are thinking of making some *Loving Truffles* for someone you find it easy to love, how about making a few extra for..?

Help us, Lord, to be less selective in those to whom we are willing to show your love;
may we learn to reach out more readily to those who need the special touch of your love today. Amen

Mardi Gras Mini Pancakes

Why not hold a Pancake Party on Shrove Tuesday as an outreach to families or young people?

Unlike traditional pancakes which are always a last-minute scramble, these can be made in advance and also freeze well. They are a reminder that Lent is about to begin and could give you the opportunity to talk about the meaning of the season with friends and neighbours.

Ingredients

110g (4oz) self-raising flour
50g (2oz) caster sugar
50g (2oz) chopped candied peel
Zest of half lemon, finely grated
1 medium egg
150ml (¼ pint) milk
Lard or oil for greasing

You will also need a griddle or heavy-based frying pan.

Method

1 Sift flour into a bowl and add sugar, candied peel and lemon zest.
2 Whisk egg and milk together and add gradually to mixture beating well.
3 Grease griddle or frying pan and cook in batches using about a tablespoon of mixture for each pancake and cooking over a medium heat for 1–2 minutes each side.
4 Cool on wire rack or keep warm in a clean tea-towel if eating immediately.

Makes 10–12

But since we belong to the day, let us be self-controlled, putting on faith
and love as a breastplate, and the hope of salvation as a helmet.
1 Thessalonians 5:8 (NIV)

Although I was brought up 'chapel', I caught the idea of giving up something for Lent from my Church of England friends and it stuck. It's not a bad discipline for someone like me who is usually a compulsive nibbler! Over the years I've managed to give up chocolate, wine, crisps and – hardest of all – cheese for the 40 days leading up to Easter. It certainly seems a much better idea than wearing sackcloth and ashes as some early Christians did!

Mardi Gras – as the day before Ash Wednesday is called in many countries – is a carnival day. Mardi Gras literally means 'fat Tuesday' and carnival means 'goodbye meat'. In Britain this day is traditionally called Shrove Tuesday because believers went to be shriven – to have their sins heard by a priest and accept whatever penance he gave them. Pancakes came into it as a way of using up the rich ingredients of butter and eggs before a time of fasting to commemorate Jesus' time in the wilderness.

Many local traditions grew up around Shrove Tuesday as people had a last fling before the period of solemnity and reflection. Games, especially football, and dancing and feasting were common, as well as pancake races. One of the most unusual traditions was Nickanan Night in the West Country when boys ran riot through villages, taking gates off their hinges and making off with anything householders hadn't managed to tie down!

Last year for our Lent course at Home Group we looked at improving the balance of our lives in a Biblical context. This included making sure we looked after ourselves and had adequate rest and play as well as work so that we were equipped to be as effective in our community as possible.

Whatever we do to make Lent special, it's not a bad idea to spend some time thinking about how to change some of our less desirable habits. Perhaps we could try replacing them with something that will bless other people and bring us closer to what the Lord wants us to be.

Lord, as we remember your time in the wilderness preparing for your unique ministry,
help us to come closer to you and to live in the faith and love that are your ideal for us. Amen

9

Primrose Spring Ring

Anyone with a spring birthday would love this pretty cake.
Or why not make it as a Mother's Day surprise
for a deserving Mum? Her children would love helping you!

To sugar-frost primrose flowers, simply use a small paintbrush to coat the top and undersides of the petals with beaten egg white, then sprinkle both sides of the flowers with caster sugar and allow to dry in a warm place, eg the airing cupboard, until firm.

Ingredients
195g (6¾oz) butter
195g (6¾oz) caster sugar
Zest of one lemon, finely grated
3 large eggs
145g (4¾oz) self-raising flour
50g (2oz) cornflour
½ teaspoon baking powder

Icing
175g (6oz) icing sugar
Juice of one lemon
A few drops of yellow food
   colouring (optional)
Decorate with fresh, artificial or
   sugar paste primroses

Method
1 Preheat the oven to gas mark 5/190°C/375°F.
2 Cream together the butter, caster sugar and lemon zest,
   until pale and fluffy.
3 Beat in the eggs one at a time, always allowing the mixture
   to become fluffy after each addition.
4 Sift together the flour, cornflour and baking powder and
   carefully fold into the creamed mixture.
5 Put into a well-greased, 23cm (9in) spring-form ring mould
   and place onto a baking tray, just in case any mixture
   escapes through the loose base.
6 Bake for 25–30 minutes or until golden and springy to
   the touch.
7 Allow to cool slightly and remove outer ring of tin.
   Ease cake from base and invert onto cooling rack.
8 When cake is completely cool, transfer to a
   cake board.
9 Mix the icing sugar with the lemon
   juice and add a drop of yellow
   colouring if desired.
10 Drizzle icing along top of
   cake and allow to run down
   the sides.
11 Decorate with silk flowers.
   Alternatively make the flowers
   from sugar paste or sugar-frost
   fresh primrose flowers (see tip).

Now the Lord God had planted a garden in the east, in Eden;
and there he put the man he had formed.
Genesis 2:8 (NIV)

Spring! What does that word conjure up for you? For me, it means stowing away all the heavy winter coats and boots and looking forward to signs of new life pushing up through the ground.

I wonder if the poet, Dorothy Frances Gurney, who wrote *'One is nearer God's heart in a garden than anywhere else on earth'*, was thinking of the Garden of Eden or was just a keen gardener herself?

I can't honestly say I'm much of a gardener, though I'm happy to do the odd bit of weeding! However, it never ceases to thrill me that the dull, unpromising little seeds or bulbs contain potential for such glorious colour later on. I love to see a cottage garden with a profusion of flowers, looking as though God just tossed a handful of seed down and they all grew together in perfect harmony.

Primroses are one of my favourite spring flowers especially in their natural setting under trees on a country lane. Recently I read that farmers used to hang primroses in their cowsheds to stop fairies from stealing the milk. I wonder why? Perhaps the tradition is derived from the folklore that suggests that primroses can help humans to see fairies!

According to the Genesis story, the first people lived in a garden long before dwellings were thought of and they lived idyllically until they spoiled their relationship with their Creator through disobedience. Jesus used the imagery of seed dying in the ground in order to produce more grain as a word-picture of his own death and resurrection and the hope we now have in spite of Adam and Eve's fall.

Gardeners or nature-lovers, who watch new life spring from seeds in the earth after the long sleep of winter, must surely recognise the hand of an intelligent Creator in those little power-packs.

Creator God, thank you for the wonder of all you have made. Help us to recognise your hand in the natural world and never to take for granted the precious cycle of life. Amen

An Easter Tree

Children will love helping to make this Easter Tree. Decorated eggs are splendid symbols of new life and hope in Jesus. This festive tree is thought to have its origins in Greece about a thousand years ago.

Draw flowers or stars onto the shell with a white wax crayon, then dip the shell in a plastic cup filled with water and a few drops of food colouring. When you extract the egg, the pattern appears in relief.

You will need

Suitable twiggy branches about 60cm high
Or for a less permanent tree, use a fresh branch just coming into leaf eg forsythia
A plant pot, plaster of Paris or polyfilla
White matt emulsion, blown eggs
Paint, felt pens, sticky paper shapes, ribbon, sequins, food colouring, glitter, wax crayons for decorating
Lengths of narrow silk ribbon to hang the eggs
Yellow florist's ribbon to curl and hang on the tree
Bodkin or needle with large eye

Method

1 Choose 2 or 3 branches with plenty of twigs and set them in a plant pot using plaster of Paris or Polyfilla. Paint the branches with white emulsion and leave overnight to dry.

2 To blow the eggs, make a hole in the top and bottom of the egg with a strong needle. You might want to use the back of a spoon to very gently 'hammer' it in.

3 Gradually enlarge the hole at one end so that it is slightly bigger than the other. Push the needle through the hole and swirl it around to break up the yolk. This will make it easier to blow the egg out of its shell.

4 Cup your mouth around the smaller hole and gently blow the egg out into a basin (and use for scrambled eggs). Blowing the egg out takes a little time and patience and a lot of 'puff'.

5 Rinse the empty shell with warm water and drain well. Carefully decorate with felt pens, sticky paper shapes, ribbon, sequins, food dye, spray paint, etc.

6 Thread a length of ribbon onto a bodkin and pass through the eggshell, tying in a knot or bow at the bottom. Tie in a loop so it can be hung on a branch.

When my daughter, Katherine, was about seven, we watched a film together on Good Friday about the Passion of Christ. Feeling that the time was right, I asked her solemnly if she would like to ask Jesus into her life and we prayed a simple prayer. Moments later Katherine said, "Mummy, can I ask the disciples in too?" and I realised my enthusiasm had been badly timed…

Children are usually deeply moved – and often disturbed – by scenes of the Crucifixion and we need to be very careful how we present the life and sacrifice of Jesus to them. We also need to recognise that, as they grow up, they will question the simple childlike faith they may have had in their early years. This is healthy and we can pray that their relationship with the Lord will be stronger for it.

The Easter Tree is a lovely way of sharing the images of new life and hope in Jesus. The egg, a pagan fertility symbol, has been adopted into Christian practice because eggs for breakfast on Easter Day literally 'break the fast' of Lent as well as symbolising new life. I like the Greek tradition of carrying a painted egg to knock against another person's egg on Easter morning with the greeting,

Christ is risen! And the tradition of rolling hard-boiled eggs down a hill on Easter Monday is thought to symbolise the rolling away of the stone from Jesus' tomb.

The lambs, which often feature on Easter cards as well as being a very familiar part of the Spring scene, are another sign of new life in both the Jewish and Christian traditions and, of course, Jesus is both the Good Shepherd and the Lamb of God.

If you know children for whom Easter only means extra chocolate, why not invite them and their family to an Easter Day service and a meal afterwards? Your Easter Tree could be an interesting starting point for sharing the real meaning of the festival that is central to the Christian faith.

At this very special time of year, Lord, help us to share the message
of new life in you with everyone we meet. Amen

Bittersweet Easter Basket

At Christmas we often prepare hampers for loved ones or house-bound friends. Why not start a new tradition and share the hope of the Easter season with the gift of an attractive basket? These delicious bittersweet chocolate biscuits can be included in the basket.

Ingredients

110g (4oz) soft margarine
50g (2oz) soft brown sugar
110g (4oz) good quality plain cooking chocolate
110g (4oz) good quality milk cooking chocolate
2 heaped tablespoons coarse-cut marmalade
175g (6oz) self-raising flour

Method

1 Preheat oven to gas mark 4/180°C/350°F. Grease and line two baking sheets.
2 Cream margarine and sugar together until light and fluffy.
3 Chop and melt plain chocolate either in the microwave or in a bowl over a pan of gently simmering water. Stir into mixture with marmalade.
4 Chop milk chocolate roughly and add to mixture.
5 Sift flour and fold into mixture.
6 Divide mixture into approximately 18 walnut-sized balls and space out on baking sheets, pressing down gently with the back of a spoon.
7 Bake for about 15 minutes or until cookies look dry. Slide off carefully with a palette knife and cool upside-down on a wire rack to allow chocolate to set.
Makes approx 18

To make the Easter basket – take a small wicker basket or fruit punnet and line it with tissue or crepe paper, shredding some to look like a nest. Arrange a selection of goodies inside, eg fresh fruit, tiny Easter eggs, fluffy chicks. Include a bag of bittersweet biscuits wrapped in cellophane. Attach an Easter card or gift tag with an appropriate message.

> (Jesus) humbled himself and became obedient to death – even death on a cross!
> Therefore God exalted him to the highest place and gave him the name that is above every name,
> that at the name of Jesus every knee should bow, in heaven and on earth and under the earth,
> and every tongue confess that Jesus Christ is Lord, to the glory of God the Father.
>
> Philippians 2:8–11 (NIV)

I once read a book called *Forever Jo* written by the family of a girl who had been killed in a road accident on her way to a Christian festival. They took great comfort in the fact that she was secure in God's loving presence though they would never see her again in this life. Bittersweet memories...

Glancing out of my kitchen window recently, I saw a cross. How odd – I'd never noticed it before. I knew I drove by it often because it was on the spire of a modern church near my home. But I'd never seen it from this angle and I was nonplussed for a moment until the light dawned. Both my husband and a neighbour had been cutting back some overgrown hedges on our boundary.

What a lesson there was in that! The cross had been there all the time, but something had been allowed to obscure it from view. It started me thinking about how the hectic pace of life can make us blind to the enduring message of the death and resurrection of Jesus. Often films portray the agony of the cross and we should never lose sight of how much it cost Jesus to hang there totally separated from his Father, bearing all the past, present and future sins of the world in our place. That is the bitter truth.

A verse from the poignant Graham Kendrick song, *Thorns in the Straw*, shows Mary almost anticipating the sorrow that was to come:

Just a blanket on the floor
Of a vacant cattle stall,
But there the child was born.
She held him in her arms
And as she laid him down to sleep
She wondered – will it always be
So bitter and so sweet.

The amazing, sweet side of the story is that, after all the anguish, Jesus rose again! And what's more, he's living and reigning with his Father in heaven and, if we believe, then we will be there with him one day.

At Easter time let's take a fresh look at the empty cross of Jesus and breathe in new hope of sharing a glorious eternity with him in heaven.

Lord, we can barely begin to imagine the agony of the cross and the total separation from your Father. But Lord, we rejoice that you overcame death not just for yourself but for all who believe in you. Praise you Jesus!

Maypole Cake

This would make an unusual cake for a May birthday.
For a little girl's party, the figures could be included in the take-home bags.

Ingredients

350g (12oz) self-raising flour
275g (10oz) caster sugar
275g (10oz) softened butter or soft margarine
5 large eggs
3 tablespoons milk
2 teaspoons vanilla essence

For icing and decorating cake:

110g (4oz) soft margarine
225g (8oz) icing sugar
1 teaspoon vanilla essence
2 tablespoons milk
Sieved apricot or strawberry jam
50g (2oz) desiccated coconut
Few drops green food colouring
Thick wooden knitting needle or
  length of dowel
Strong glue or double-
  sided tape
6 x 0.5m (½yd) lengths
  of coloured narrow
  ribbon
6 toy figures
  such as *Duplo*
  or *Sylvanian*
  Families
Wide ribbon

Method

1 Preheat oven to gas mark 3/170°C/325°F. Grease and line a 23cm (9in) round spring-form or loose-bottomed cake tin.
2 Sift flour into large bowl and add all other cake ingredients. Using a food processor or electric whisk, blend all the ingredients together for at least a minute until a smooth batter is formed. Spoon mixture into tin and level the top making a slight indentation in centre.
3 Bake in centre of oven for 1¼–1½ hours until cake is golden and a skewer inserted in middle comes out clean.
4 Leave in tin for 10 minutes then cool on wire rack.

Instructions to complete cake

1 Beat margarine with sieved icing sugar, vanilla essence and a few drops of milk to make spreading consistency.
2 Slice cake into 2 horizontal layers.
3 Use half the icing, together with jam, to sandwich the layers together and spread rest on top.
4 Place desiccated coconut in a small plastic bag with a few drops of green food colouring and shake until evenly coloured. Spread on top of cake to represent grass.
5 Attach ribbons to top of knitting needle with glue or double-sided tape and weave or twist them a couple of times. Insert needle into centre of cake and attach ends of ribbons to figures with a blob of icing sugar or Blu Tack.
6 Wrap band or ribbon round cake.

There is a time for everything, and a season for every activity under heaven...
a time to plant and a time to uproot...

Ecclesiastes 3:1–2 (NIV)

It was a highlight of the year at my Primary School. The teacher would choose two sturdy boys to stand back-to-back at the base of the maypole holding it steady while circles of girls and boys wove their ribbons in and out in the hope of tying them up! It never happened of course, as when the plait got halfway down the teacher would call out for us to change direction and undo it again. It was great fun though!

Mayday celebrations have their origins in pagan festivities when the ancient Celts used to celebrate the first spring planting after the long winter. As a Christian, I don't have a problem with that as I recognise it as worship of the Unseen Force who was in control of the seasons before Jesus came to show us just how personal that Creator God is. When Christianity reached our shores, it must have seemed like a huge piece of the jigsaw fitting into place for many who had been wondering!

In the Middle Ages, the church frowned on such jollities as the Queen of the May but later it would absorb many pagan rites specifically to win over converts.

At one time every village in England had a maypole festooned with ribbons and flowers to welcome the spring. It was a great honour at the high Anglican church, where I attended Youth Club, to be chosen as Flower Queen for the year. This Mayday festival had close connections with the Virgin Mary, to whom the month of May is dedicated, and I remember it as a really joyful religious occasion with special hymns.

So let's affirm our long-standing traditions whilst recognising that the coming of Christianity put a new perspective on the cycle of the seasons and assured us that God is in charge of 'all the changing scenes of life'.

God of the changing seasons, teach me to dance to the rhythm
of life and to see your hand in all creation. Amen

17

Wendy's Caring Cake

I have several diabetic or dieting friends who hate to be left out when sweet goodies are being served. Wendy, who baked several of the recipes for our photo shoot, gave me this wonderful recipe. The cake has no added sugar and just a little oil so it is a relatively healthy treat for those who need some extra tender loving care.

 The ratio of juice to pineapple in the tin can vary from one brand to another so, if the mixture is quite wet, add an extra tablespoon of flour or, if it is a little too dry, add one or two tablespoons of milk.

Ingredients

425g (15oz) can crushed pineapple in natural juice
450g (1lb) mixed dried fruit
1 teaspoon mixed spice
4 tablespoons corn or vegetable oil
2 medium eggs
225g (8oz) self-raising wholemeal flour
(or 225g (8oz) plain wholemeal flour and
   3 teaspoons baking powder)

Method

1 Place pineapple (including juice), dried fruit, spice and oil in a medium saucepan. Bring slowly to the boil and simmer for three minutes. Turn into a bowl, cover and leave overnight or until completely cold.
2 Preheat oven to gas mark 5/190°C/375°F. Grease an 18cm (7in) round cake tin, or a 907g (2lb) loaf tin.
3 Add flour and beaten eggs to the cold mixture and stir well until thoroughly mixed.
4 Place mixture in tin, cover top loosely with foil and bake for 1 hour. Remove foil and continue baking for approximately ½ hour longer or until a skewer inserted in the middle comes out clean.
5 Cool in tin.

Cuts into 12 slices

> He went to him and bandaged his wounds, pouring on oil and wine.
> Then he put the man on his own donkey, brought him to an inn and took care of him.
>
> Luke 10:34 (NIV)

I love the story of the Good Samaritan – it's so graphic. Also, sadly, it's true that in this day and age we are equally willing to pass by on the other side and let someone else sort out the problem. In this case, someone who would have been considered a social outcast by the injured man's own people.

There are people crying out for our care all around us and sometimes we have to put ourselves in their shoes to know just how to meet their needs.

One New Year's Eve I had organised a party at Church but it began snowing quite heavily early in the evening and, after phoning one or two people, I decided to cancel it. Most people were relieved, especially those who would have had to travel several miles by car. But some of my single friends were devastated. "We could have walked there and stayed the night if necessary!" one exclaimed, and I recognised the fact that to be on her own that night was far worse than any physical discomfort she might have felt.

I often wince when much is made of Mother's or Father's Day in churches where there are people who would have loved to be parents if only circumstances had been different. And I say that as the single parent of a child whose father was completely absent. How sensitive we need to be towards others...

The Samaritan had nothing to gain by his good-heartedness but the satisfaction of knowing he had helped out in a crisis. And look at how he helped! First, he got his hands dirty cleaning the man up. Then, after using his own transport to carry him to the inn, he stayed with him, no doubt offering comfort and reassurance as well as medical attention. And when he had to leave, he made sure there was someone well-paid to continue with the care.

It may only be making the right kind of food for someone with special dietary needs or it may be showing real sacrificial love in terms of our time and resources but, whatever we do, we'll be doing it for Jesus. And Jesus said, "Whatever you did for one of the least of these brothers of mine, you did it for me." (Matthew 25:40 NIV)

Lord, sometimes I just don't feel like being the Good Samaritan you want me to be.
Forgive me and help me to recognise the needs of others in a more sympathetic way. Amen

Rumba Jumbles

The name of these jolly little biscuits was inspired by Pam, a new friend from my ballroom-and-sequence dancing class. The rum can be replaced with orange juice.

Ingredients

75g (3oz) raisins
2 tablespoons dark rum
110g (4oz) butter or margarine
65g (2½oz) granulated sugar
1 medium egg yolk
175g (6oz) plain flour
1 heaped teaspoon cinnamon
Demerara sugar (optional)
Plain chocolate for coating

Method

1 Soak the raisins in the rum in a small bowl for a couple of hours, stirring occasionally.
2 Cream the butter and sugar together until light and fluffy.
3 Beat in the egg yolk.
4 Sieve the flour and cinnamon together and add to mixture with raisins and any remaining rum to make a stiff dough.
5 Turn onto a lightly floured board and roll into a 5cm (2in) sausage shape. Flatten slightly, then wrap in cling film and chill in fridge for at least an hour.
6 Preheat oven to gas mark 4/180°C/350°F. Lightly grease a baking sheet.
7 Using a serrated knife, cut slices approx ½cm (¼in) thick and lay on baking sheet, shaping into ovals. Sprinkle with Demerara sugar if liked.
8 Bake for about 15 minutes until golden.
9 Allow to cool on the baking sheet for a couple of minutes then transfer to a wire rack.
10 Half coat with chocolate for a luxurious finish.
Makes about 18

Soon after I first met my husband, Ern, he took me to the Tower Ballroom in Blackpool and tried to waltz me round the floor. Hopeless! In spite of loving a good Barn Dance, this ballroom stuff reduced me to a clumsy idiot.

So, at the beginning of this year, inspired by those TV programmes that make it look so effortless, we decided to take some lessons in ballroom and sequence along with our good friends, Helen and Dave. Hmm... Ern was confident that he would soon brush up the skills he'd learned as a young man and I was certain to become Queen of the Ballroom in no time...

Umm – not quite. I hated the first few lessons! It wasn't that I had no sense of rhythm – I do conduct a choir, after all – nor that my feet wouldn't do what my brain told them. No, my problem was memory.
I was fine while I was following Anne, the patient teacher, but as soon as we set off on our own, I simply couldn't remember what came next. Far from performing a recognisable Rumba One (never mind a Melody Foxtrot or Spindle Swing), I could only produce a stumbling Rumba Jumble...

Time after time I would cry, "But I can't remember the sequence! I can't see the pattern!"

We were often relegated to the bottom of the class and taken on one side for individual tuition. Meanwhile, Helen and Dave rapidly rose in the ranks and were soon sailing round the floor like professionals.

When Jesus said, "Whoever exalts himself will be humbled" (Matthew 23:12), I don't suppose he had my dancing in mind. But, I learned a valuable lesson in humility, and if you care to come along any Monday evening, our efforts may still provide you with tear-jerking entertainment!

Lord, help us to realise our limitations and to accept our strengths and needs.
Thank you that we can enjoy learning from each other. Amen

Man-sized Munchies

Socks and hankies – forget them! Most men will appreciate a version
of this gift if it includes some of their favourite cheese.
Too good to keep exclusively for the men though!

Replace mustard with heaped teaspoon
of *Marmite*. Use other kinds of nuts as
preferred. Peanuts work well.

When cool, wrap munchies together with
a waxed cheese in a large sheet of
cellophane. Finish with a coloured ribbon
and a gift card.

Ingredients

75g (3oz) butter or margarine
110g (4oz) mature cheddar cheese, grated
1 large egg, beaten
85ml (3fl oz) milk
1 heaped teaspoon wholegrain mustard
225g (8oz) porridge oats
75g (3oz) walnuts, chopped
A little extra cheese for decoration

Method

1 Preheat oven to gas mark 4/180°C/350°F. Lightly grease
  18cm (7in) square cake tin.
2 Melt the butter or margarine in a large saucepan. Remove
  from heat and stir in grated cheese, egg, milk and mustard
  until well blended
3 Stir in oats and walnuts.
4 Place mixture in tin and level the surface.
5 Sprinkle a little finely grated cheese over the top.
6 Bake for about 30 minutes until golden.
7 Cool in tin, then cut into 9 squares.
  Remember! Cheese needs to be kept in
  the fridge.

To make mini munchies for a party,
cut into 36 small squares and decorate
with a swirl of cream cheese and nuts
or a slice of tomato.

I've got to say it – I believe men should be men and women should be women! In this day and age, it's not politically correct to admit to women being 'the weaker sex' in spite of obvious physical differences. But think of how nature has created the woman to be the nurturer as she carries the unborn baby and the man to be the provider and protector. Any portrayal of the Holy Family on a Christmas card reinforces this, as Mary cradles the baby Jesus and Joseph stands guard over them.

In the beginning, God created man and then woman to be his companion (Genesis 2). Jesus came to earth as a *man* and he recognised that while men and women were equal in the sight of God, they had different roles to play. I'm sure we could have a lively debate on this subject!

As a single parent in particularly difficult circumstances, I had to be Mum and Dad to Katherine, but I know how far from God's ideal it was.

Later, when I married Ern, it took me a while to get used to the idea that I didn't have to struggle in with the heavy shopping all by myself but that he would like the occasional button sewn on, please! Nowadays, through our circumstances, he does all the washing and I do all the long-distance driving – and that's what suits us, so I am far from thinking we have to stick rigidly to traditional male-female roles!

As you make these Munchies, think about the roles of the men and women in your circle and whether they complement each other just as God intended at the beginning of Creation...

Lord, help us to be secure in our identity and to know what roles you
intend us to play. Show us how to get the balance of life right
and to be there for each other to provide care and support. Amen

Honey Buns

These easy-to-make little buns are perfect at teatime.
For an interesting gift for someone with a sweet tooth, wrap
some up with a jar of special honey and a honey drizzler.
Add a bee-shaped gift tag just for fun!

 The buns freeze well, but also improve,
becoming even more sticky and moist,
if kept in a tin for a couple of days.

Ingredients
200g (7oz) self-raising flour
150g (5oz) soft margarine
110g (4oz) light soft brown sugar
2 medium eggs
4 tablespoons thick set honey
1 tablespoon boiling water
25g (1oz) flaked almonds
Icing sugar for dusting

Method
1 Preheat oven to gas mark 4/180°C/350°F. Prepare bun tins
with 18 paper cases.
2 Place all ingredients except almonds in a large bowl and
beat together for several minutes until completely blended.
Alternatively use a food processor.
3 Divide mixture between paper cases and sprinkle flaked
almonds on top of each.
4 Bake near top of oven for about 15 minutes. Cool on a
wire rack.
Makes 18 buns.

A young girl that I know was very distressed by verbal bullying at school. She found some comfort in a poem by Barrie Wade which claimed that the old saying, *Sticks and stones may break my bones but words will never hurt me,* was not true and that spiteful words would remain in the memory long after physical scars had faded. The third verse was particularly helpful as she realised that others felt as she did:

Pain from words has left its scar
On mind and heart that's tender.
Cuts and bruises now have healed:
It's words that I remember.

Eventually she came to terms with the bullying and moved on.

As a teenager, my Bible Class teacher impressed me when she said her father always 'spat out his words and looked at them' before he spoke. She wanted us to understand the importance of thinking before we speak. I knew I would never live up to this and, to this day, I am not known for my tact and diplomacy in all situations! It is difficult when you are an impulsive person not to say just what is on your mind without regard for the others' feelings, but we should keep trying.

The choir I lead is currently rehearsing Roger Jones' wonderful musical *Jailbreak*, which tells the story of Paul and Silas in prison at Philippi. The song *Dangerous Words*, suggests that God's word is 'dangerous' because it challenges us to change our way of thinking. If we start trusting him in every area of life then it may feel, for a while, that we are not in control of our own lives. But only when we truly learn to lean on him will we see his real power.

Our use of words sets us apart from the other animals – let's be sure our words are like honey and use these powerful tools only for good.

PS Did you know that honey bees gather nectar from two million flowers just to make one 500g (1lb) jar of honey?

Peace and Joy Pentecost Pasties

Pentecost, the time when God's Spirit was sent to the disciples to empower them to spread the gospel after Jesus had ascended to heaven, is not one of our better-known times for celebration. This recipe is ideal for a family picnic and its name was suggested by our nine-year-old granddaughter, Katherine.

Ingredients

1 medium onion
250g (9oz) fresh, lean minced beef
1 large potato, boiled and diced
1 medium carrot, boiled and diced
150ml (¼ pint) thick gravy
1 level tablespoon fresh chopped parsley
1 x 375g (13oz) pack ready-rolled
  shortcrust pastry, or use own recipe
A little beaten egg to glaze (optional)

Method

1 Chop and fry the onion in a little oil. Add mince and cook until just brown.
2 Add diced potato and carrot (you could use leftovers).
3 Fold in gravy and parsley and set aside.
4 Carefully unroll pastry and, using a small plate as a guide, cut 6 circles. Reserve pastry trimmings.
5 Divide meat and vegetable mixture between the 6 circles, dampen edges and fold over to make pasties, crimping the edges with the back of a fork. Place pasties on a lightly greased baking sheet.
6 From the trimmings cut 6 dove shapes. Then, with kitchen scissors, cut wavy flames. Arrange doves and flames on each pasty, using beaten egg or water to help them adhere.
7 Brush doves and flames with beaten egg to give them a glaze and help them to stand out.
8 Bake at gas mark 5/190°C/375°F for about 20 minutes until golden. Serve hot or cold.

Makes 6 pasties

When the day of Pentecost came, they were all together in one place. Suddenly a sound
like the blowing of a violent wind came from heaven…They saw what seemed to be tongues of fire
that separated and came to rest on each of them. All of them were filled with the Holy Spirit
and began to speak in other tongues as the Spirit enabled them.

Acts 2:1–4 (NIV)

We used to call it 'The Treats'. On Whit Saturday all the Sunday Schools in the area would parade through the streets behind a brass band, stopping every so often to sing rousing hymns.

Our huge banner, showing the Parable of the Sower, was carried on poles by two young men and the year I was chosen to hold one of the streamers that kept it steady was a very proud one. When the Procession of Witness was over we went to a school field for games and tea with ice-cream and pop – a real treat.

Pentecost, or Whit Sunday, celebrates the birth of the Church after Jesus, the man, had returned to Heaven. It was encouraging to hear of a Primary school where children were helped to understand the coming of the Holy Spirit by making cardboard bands to fit around their heads with paper 'tongues of fire' attached. So many schools fail to teach the real truths of Christianity today.

It's a difficult concept at any age, understanding how the disciples were empowered by the Spirit – the third member of the Trinity – so that they could take the good news of Jesus to all corners of the earth. But, as they experienced that supernatural event, they must have remembered Jesus' promise that they would know a deep peace and joy which would equip them for the task of spreading the gospel.

When we enjoyed 'The Treats', we had little idea of the meaning behind the special day. It was just a wonderful occasion with lots of fun. Still, what better way to celebrate the momentous birth of the Christian Church?

Thank you, Father, for the gift of your Holy Spirit as our guide, our comforter and our friend.
Help us to share the power of your Spirit with everyone we meet. Amen

Grace Stones

The tradition of giving thanks before a meal has largely died out. Why not revive it by placing a Grace Stone on the table and inviting someone to read it aloud?

You will need:

Smooth, well-shaped pebbles, clean and dry
Tester pots of pastel emulsion paints
  (or leftover emulsion)
Fine waterproof black pen
Enamel modelling paints and fine brushes
Or scraps from découpage or card-making and
  strong glue
Matt modelling varnish (optional)

Instructions

1 Give pebbles two coats of emulsion, allowing them to dry between coats.
2 Write a Grace on the best surface of the pebble with the waterproof pen (see ideas on page 29).
3 Either draw a pattern with a soft pencil then paint with enamels or decorate with découpage scraps.
4 When dry, varnish for a more durable finish (optional)

> The Lord Jesus…took bread, and when he had given thanks, he broke it…
>
> 1 Corinthians 11:23–24 (NIV)

I know of a lively Youth Club where the members unashamedly sing a Grace, accompanied by actions, to the well-known tune from the film *The Addams Family* before a meal in a fast-food restaurant. What a witness! Here's how it goes:

Da da da da, click click
Da da da da, click click…

Oh Lord we're really grateful
For every cup and plateful,
Forgive us when we're wasteful
For we're your family!

You clothe us and you feed us,
You guide us and you lead us
To live and love like Jesus
For we're you're family!

The practice of saying Grace was once taken for granted in most households but now it can come as a surprise to unsuspecting guests! Just placing a Grace Stone on a meal table can be a great conversation starter.

Here's a selection of Graces to start you off, but you may know of others and there are plenty of books available to give you ideas:

We have food, the table's spread;
thank you, God, who gave us bread.

For health and strength and daily food,
we praise your name, O Lord.
(Traditional)

For our food and those who prepare it;
for health and strength and friends to share it;
we say thank you, Lord. (Anon)

God bless this bunch as they munch their lunch.

As Jesus blessed the loaves and fishes, bless to us these modern dishes.

For food and friends and fellowship, we give you thanks, dear Lord.

Lord, may we never take for granted the grace you pour on us every day.
Keep us alert to how we can share your goodness with others. Amen

Ginger Fruit Jubilees

✓ Use half and half, white and plain chocolate, for added variety.

I often find that older people celebrating anniversaries don't want yet more knick-knacks as gifts. These unusual petit-fours, arranged in a box appropriately coloured to match the occasion, make a thoughtful change. They are packed with healthy fruit and nuts which help to cancel out the chocolate shells!

Ingredients

110g (4oz) margarine
110g (4oz) golden syrup
175g (6oz) ready-to-eat dried apricots, chopped
75g (3oz) raisins
110g (4oz) almonds, brazils or mixed nuts, chopped
175g (6oz) ginger biscuits, crushed
200g (7oz) good quality plain cooking chocolate

Method

1 Melt margarine and syrup in a pan over a medium heat. Bring to boil and simmer for a couple of minutes, stirring. Remove from heat.
2 In a large bowl mix dried fruit, nuts and biscuits, then pour toffee mixture over and blend well.
3 When cool, cover bowl with cling film and leave in fridge for several hours or overnight.
4 Divide mixture into 36 balls. Melt chocolate and dip each ball in, using a fork to lift out. Set on baking parchment or greaseproof paper.
5 Present in individual sweet cases.

Makes 36 petit fours

It shall be a jubilee for you; each one of you is to return to his family property and each to his own clan.

Leviticus 25:10 (NIV)

Special anniversaries, such as Silver, Ruby and Golden, mark the passage of time and are an opportunity to say thanks for God's goodness through the years. My parents celebrated their Ruby Anniversary with a church service at which my brother read the lesson and I sang a solo. Afterwards, the whole congregation joined family and friends for party food. The memories of this sustained my Mum through the date of their Golden Anniversary when Dad was no longer with us.

In an age when marriage appears to be a throwaway commodity, it's great to get family and friends together in one place to celebrate long-lasting relationships where a couple have stayed together through all the ups and downs of life.

The meaning of the word 'jubilee' is uncertain but it is thought to originate from the Hebrew for the ram's-horn trumpet with which the jubilee was proclaimed.

The Israelites had been given a command by the Lord to make each 50th year special. It would be a year when families returned to their roots, all debts were cancelled and the land was given a rest from intensive farming. These three ideas make such good sense.

As the original jubilee was a time to cancel debts, maybe an anniversary would be a good time to bury any hatchets too? It's just a thought... And to fulfil the third part, why not find a way of helping farmers in the developing world to manage their land more effectively, perhaps through better water supplies or equipment? Several couples I know have asked for donations to good causes instead of gifts at their anniversaries, and that seems like a very special way of thanking God for all his goodness to us.

Lord, just as we sing 'Jubilate everybody!' we want to praise you
for all the good things that we can celebrate. Thank you, generous God. Amen

Blueberry Birthday Buns

Some friends might appreciate these special little buns instead of a whole birthday cake. They are great for sharing in a workplace or on a picnic. They were suggested by our granddaughter, Sophie. Arrange a few on a doiley with candles in the centre of one or two for a thoughtful gift.

 Try these buns served warm with clotted cream – delicious!

 Dried blueberries can be used when fresh are not available. Dried ready-to-eat cranberries also make a good alternative and go down well at Christmas.

Ingredients
110g (4oz) soft margarine
75g (3oz) caster sugar
2 medium eggs
110g (4oz) self-raising flour
125g (4½oz) fresh blueberries

Method
1 Preheat oven to gas mark 6/200°C/400°F. Place 6 paper muffin cases in a muffin tin.
2 Cream margarine with sugar until light and fluffy.
3 Beat eggs together then add to the mixture with flour and blueberries, folding together lightly. Do not over-mix.
4 Divide mixture between paper cases and bake for 20–25 minutes or until well-risen and golden.
5 Cool on a wire rack.
Makes 6 large buns

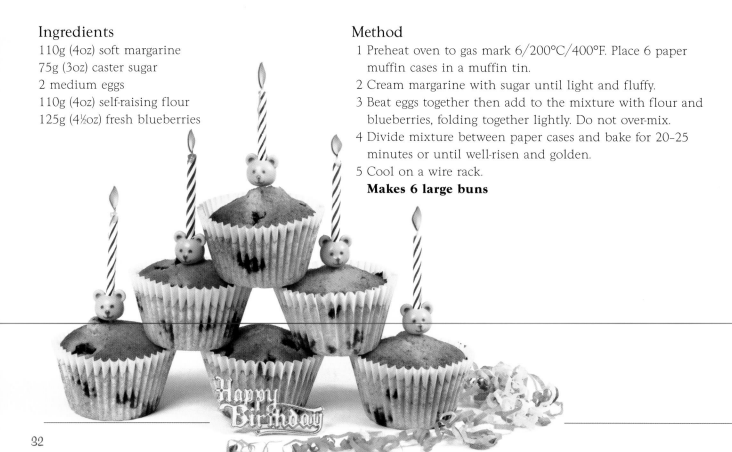

> Each year (Samuel's) mother made him a little robe and took it to him
> when she went up with her husband to offer the annual sacrifice.
>
> 1 Samuel 2:19 (NIV)

'We're inviting you to a Naughty Party,' I heard my former minister announce over the phone. Some minutes later I understood that several people at their new church had birthdays ending with a nought and were holding a joint *Noughties* celebration!

As a young teenager, I was given a Birthday Book and went round the staff and prefects at school asking them to write their names in the appropriate dates. All agreed except one – a strict old martinet of a music teacher. "I don't have birthdays anymore, child," she said with her sweet but severe smile, and signed her name in a margin instead. Even as a teenager that struck me as so sad. I knew she was a single person living in a rented room and probably had no-one to remember her on that special day.

If I'd been older and wiser I might have made more effort – even given her an un-birthday present at some point, although I could imagine her refusing it and ticking me off into the bargain.

Birthdays don't seem to feature very much in the Bible but, of course, Salome asked for the gruesome gift of John the Baptist's head on Herod's special day (Matthew 14:7) and, in the Old Testament, Pharaoh had an odd way of celebrating too (look it up in Genesis 40:20–23)! But I like to think of Hannah's annual gift of a new robe for her little son Samuel, whom she had wanted so badly, as a sort of birthday present. Samuel went to the temple to serve Eli, the priest, at a very tender age and after that they only saw each other once a year. How they must have looked forward to that day!

Marking the passage of time, acknowledging the gift of another year of life with its ups and down, is important to most of us. There are people today in our own neighbourhoods, churches and circles of friends, who may dread birthdays as their loved ones pass away and the cards and greetings get fewer and fewer. Let's be sure that we mark their special days with them, as well as including them in our own celebrations.

> We know we are all special to you, Lord, and we thank you for friends and families
> who make us feel special too. Help us to be sensitive to the needs of those who don't
> have close family with whom they can share important days. Amen

Bags of Fun and Peppermint Creams

"Are we nearly there yet?" It's a cliché – but every generation of children uses that plaintive wail when bored on a journey. These exciting bags are a novel gift for children facing a long trip. Peppermint creams can also help since the fragrance and flavour of peppermint is recommended to alleviate travel sickness.

Ingredients

250g (9oz) icing sugar
1½ tablespoons milk
A few drops of peppermint essence
A drop of green food colouring (optional)
Paper sweet cases
Granulated sugar

Method

1 Sift icing sugar into a bowl, add milk and a few drops of peppermint essence. Mix with a wooden spoon until mixture binds together and has the texture of *Plasticine*. If too wet, add a little more icing sugar; if too stiff, add a few drops of milk.

2 To make green and white sweets, divide the mixture in half and add a drop of green food colouring to one half.

3 Shape the mixture into small balls, about the size of a marble, roll in granulated sugar and place in sweet cases; or roll out a long 'sausage' of mixture and cut into slices. Turn each sweet in sugar and leave on a plate to harden.

4 A simple presentation box can be made by covering a cheese triangle box in attractive paper.

Makes about 20 to 22 sweets

For the Bags of Fun you will need:

A bag for each child and a selection of the following ideas – each wrapped separately:

A tiny notebook and pen; I-Spy type book; metal puzzles to disentangle; a length of string to play Cat's Cradle; a list of 20 things to look for with points for each eg 1 point for a cow, 2 for a helicopter; French knitting bobbin and wool...

The rule is that only one item can be unwrapped every half hour. Hopefully some items will occupy children for longer! When my daughter, Katherine, was 10 we travelled to Scotland together and I hid the parcels under her seat. She loved the idea of feeling for another little surprise whenever she was a bit fed-up. Adapt the idea to suit your own situation and try the 'Pound Shops' for inspiration!

...Jesus, tired as he was from the journey, sat down by the well.

John 4:6 (NIV)

Dad, although he was usually a good driver, didn't always get it right. Late one wet winter night, we arrived in Blackpool for a weekend visit to my grandparents – and ended up with the front bumper jammed on a 'Keep Left' sign.

"But I was following the tramlines," my bemused father explained to the policeman. "Yes sir," came the tart reply. "But you're not a tram, are you?"

He was let off with a caution, but it was another lesson that we need to follow the road marked out for us and not deviate onto a route we were never meant to take!

Journeys can be tiring, boring and frustrating but, to get from A to B, they are a necessity. Journeys can also be stimulating and exciting, and provide great opportunities for experiences even before we reach our destination. If Jesus hadn't sat down to rest beside the well on his journey through Samaria, he might have missed the chance to tell the woman about the living water that could change her life!

I was tempted to call this piece 'Journeying Mercies' as I know how pleased parents will be to have something different to occupy their children! As a child, I used to suffer quite badly from car sickness and I am grateful in retrospect to my Dad who devised new Number Plate and I-Spy games as he drove along.

Encouraging children – and adults – to be observant as they travel, not only makes the journey easier but can also be an object lesson for the journey of life. Satellite Navigation may have made finding obscure places easier, but for me there's nothing like the thrill of reading a map. Studying God's word every day may take more effort than just listening to a sermon once a week but we need both if we are to progress on the route that God has planned for us.

One more step along the world I go, one more step along the world I go,
From the old world to the new, keep me travelling along with You!
(Sydney Carter – copyright Stainer and Bell)

Perfect Playdough

This is good to give to a Mum with younger children left at home after the others have gone back to school. It would also make an excellent gift for your church crèche or toddler group.

Obviously small children should be discouraged from tasting the dough, but the strong flavour of salt and cream of tartar usually means that they only try it once!

You will need:
250g (9oz) plain flour
2 tablespoons cream of tartar
350ml (12fl oz) water
150g (5oz) salt
1 tablesoon oil
A few drops of food colouring
A mini rolling pin and set of children's
    biscuit cutters
Glitter (optional)

Method
1 Mix together the flour and cream of tartar in a bowl.
2 Boil the water, salt and oil in a saucepan.
3 Stir the liquid into the flour, adding a few drops of food colouring as you do so. If you want playdough in two different colours, put half the mixture into each of two bowls before adding the colouring.
4 Allow the mixture to cool a little before kneading it well so that it becomes smooth and flexible.
5 As an optional extra, add a little glitter to the dough to create an interesting effect.
6 Cool dough completely before letting children play with it.
7 If you wrap the playdough in cling film and then a polythene bag, it will keep in the fridge for several weeks.

The city streets will be filled with boys and girls playing there.

Zechariah 8:5 (NIV)

"It is a happy talent to know how to play," said the philosopher and poet, Ralph Waldo Emerson.

Play is one of the main ways children learn to understand the world around them. We can teach functional skills like numeracy and literacy, but coping skills such as self-confidence, self-control and compassion are best learned through play.

I was surprised to hear on the radio recently that DVDs, designed to help young babies develop, are being used by mothers. They put their babies in front of the television because they don't know how to play with, or even what to say to, their children.

By contrast, in the novel *Blessings* by Anna Quindlen, a young man finds a new-born baby on his doorstep and decides to look after it. Although, at first, he feels foolish pulling faces and babbling as the baby book suggests, he soon finds enormous pleasure from the child's reactions and she begins to thrive as a healthy individual.

One of my fridge magnets says *The best thing to give children is time*. Whether it's action rhymes with a toddler or a board game with older children, our involvement in some of their play can only help their development. On a Wednesday afternoon at our house, you will usually find us playing word games round the table after tea – and it's often Granddad who comes up with the funniest ideas! We value this brief time with the grandchildren especially as we realise they will soon be teenagers and such frivolities will be beneath them.

Although we don't always call it play, adults' leisure time is also essential to well-being. From aquarobics to dominoes, line-dancing to Beetle Drives, enjoying ourselves in the company of others helps us to stay young at heart. The writer Mark Twain said, "Work consists of whatever a body is obliged to do. Play consists of whatever a body is not obliged to do!"

Let's never lose the gift of having fun!

Thank you, Father, for the innocence of childhood and the joy of play.
Help us to keep that childlike sense of wonder at all you have given us. Amen

Easy-Peasy Autumn Chutney

No cooking is involved in this delicious chutney which is very agreeable with Harvest Pinwheels (see page 42) and some tasty cheese. It keeps well for a few weeks and would make a good addition to a Christmas hamper too.

If the mixture seems too wet after 24 hours, add an extra handful of raisins to soak up any remaining vinegar.

The recipe made the three jars in the photo, with some over.

Keeps for at least a month.
Once opened, keep in fridge.

Ingredients

225g (8oz) raisins
225g (8oz) sultanas
225g (8oz) cooking apples
225g (8oz) onions
225g (8oz) dark soft brown or granulated sugar
½ teaspoon salt
Pinch of pepper
284ml (½ pint)
  malt vinegar

Method

1 Chop the raisins and sultanas and mince or finely grate the apples and onions into a large bowl. (If you have a food processor, use this to grate all the ingredients.)
2 Stir in the sugar and add salt and pepper.
3 Pour over the vinegar, cover and leave in the fridge for 24 hours, stirring occasionally.
4 Spoon the chutney into washed and sterilised jars. Cover with a wax disc and a plastic lined screw top lid.
5 Label and finish jars with material 'hat' if liked.

> Take my yoke upon you and learn from me, for I am gentle and humble in heart,
> and you will find rest for your souls. For my yoke is easy and my burden is light.
> Matthew 11:29–30 (NIV)

Easy-peasy, lemon-squeezy, the young children I taught used to chant when they were scornful of another child's failure at some task. When children use the term *easy-peasy* they mean that something is very straightforward and they are confident that they will have no difficulty with it.

On a website that asked for the adult equivalent to this phrase, various responses were:

Easy as pie!
Piece of cake!
It's a breeze!
A walk in the park!

And what does Jesus say? If we yoke ourselves to him, we will find life so much easier. Then, when difficult days do come along, Jesus is there to help us with the struggle.

The modern translation of Jesus' words puts it this way: *Walk with me and work with me – watch how I do it. Learn the unforced rhythms of grace. I won't lay anything heavy or ill-fitting on you. Keep company with me and you'll learn to live freely and lightly.* (The Message)

If only I could learn to live freely and lightly instead of trying to prove something all the time! Many of us are driven by a voice from childhood – perhaps a parent or a teacher – telling us we have constantly to try harder or we won't make the grade. We sometimes hear of the most sincere Christians suffering burnout as they overtax themselves, thinking they have to be everything to everybody all the time.

But Jesus says the opposite. He already loves us and accepts us just as we are and all he wants is for us to follow his example and live an effective, balanced life. He knew just what his Father was calling him to do at any given time and he also knew when he needed to take a break and rest.

While you are making this easy-peasy chutney, why not think about that telling little phrase, *Let go and let God?*

Lord, we are sorry for the times when we make things more difficult
than you intended them to be. Help us to recognise the simplicity of
working with, rather than for, you. Amen

Eve's Temptation

When cooking apples are being given away by the bagful by friends and neighbours with over-laden trees, I like to make this scrumptious, very moist cake which can also be served warm as a pudding with clotted cream or crème fraîche.

Ingredients

150ml (¼ pint) cider or apple juice
225g (8oz) sultanas
110g (4oz) butter or margarine
110g (4oz) light soft brown sugar
2 medium eggs
1 large cooking apple
225g (8oz) self-raising flour
1 level teaspoon mixed spice
Icing sugar for dusting

Method

1 Soak sultanas in cider/apple juice overnight in covered dish.
2 Preheat oven to gas mark 4/180°C/350°F. Grease and line a medium-sized roasting tin or deep rectangular cake tin.
3 Cream butter and sugar together until light and fluffy.
4 Beat in eggs with a little flour to prevent curdling.
5 Peel, core and chop apple and stir in with sultanas and cider.
6 Sift flour and spice together and fold into mixture.
7 Turn into tin, level the surface and bake for approximately 1 hour or until well risen and firm to the touch.
8 Leave to cool in tin, then turn out and cut into squares.
This cake freezes well or will keep in the fridge for about three days.
Makes 16 slices

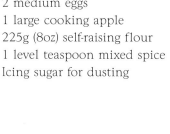

No temptation has seized you except what is common to man.
And God is faithful; he will not let you be tempted beyond what you can bear.
1 Corinthians 10:13 (NIV)

Someone once said, "Those who flee temptation usually leave a forwarding address!" When I named this cake, *Eve's Temptation*, I was thinking of how attractive the things that tempt us often seem. One delicious slice of the cake with clotted cream may be fine but, if we are tempted to eat the lot at one sitting, then not only are we being selfish in not sharing it but also we are abusing our own bodies. I have always been a bit short of willpower and I have concluded that I have a compulsive nature, so it is harder for me to win the battles... well, that's my excuse anyway...

It is not always the obvious 'big' sins like stealing or adultery that tempt us in everyday life. Aren't you ever tempted to pass on a juicy piece of gossip? To fantasise about a TV hero? Or to make a long personal call on the office phone? Think about it for a moment. Your battles with temptation may be very different to mine, but if we are open to the Lord, he will continue to help us fight our battles and refine us in the process.

Whether it's eating more than we need or spreading a rumour, missing a mid-week meeting because we are not fond of the speaker or choosing to ignore someone on her own while we chat to our best friend – let's make a bit more effort to resist temptation and see where it leads us.

I'll let John Bunyan, that wise author who, when he was imprisoned for preaching without a licence, used his time to write the classic novel, *Pilgrim's Progress*, have the last word:

Temptations, when we first meet them, are like a lion that roared at Samson; but if we can overcome them, the next time we see them we shall find a nest of honey within them.

Lord, we make all sorts of excuses for giving in to temptation. Remind us of your example in Jesus who was tempted in far greater ways than we ever will be and yet overcame them all to be our Saviour. Amen

41

Harvest Pinwheels

These savoury scones are delicious at the Harvest Supper or served warm with soup, cheese and pickles for an autumn lunch with friends.

Ingredients

Filling:
110g (4oz) butter or margarine
2 rounded teaspoons Marmite

Dough:
450g (1lb) self-raising flour
1 teaspoon mustard powder
1 teaspoon salt
110g (4oz) block margarine
110g (4oz) strong cheddar cheese, finely grated
275ml (½ pint) milk

Method

1 Preheat oven to gas mark 7/220°C/425°F. Lightly grease a 28cm x 17.5cm (11in x 7in) Swiss roll tin.
2 Cream butter or margarine with Marmite in a small bowl for the filling.
3 Sift flour, mustard and salt into a large bowl.
4 Rub in margarine. Mix in cheese.
5 Add milk and stir with fork until just mixed.
6 Knead dough lightly on a floured board. Roll half dough to rectangle approximately 34cm x 23cm (14in x 9in). Spread with half the filling and roll up from the short end. Repeat with remaining dough and filling.
7 Cut each roll into approx 2cm (1in) slices and place side by side in the tin.
8 Bake for approx 20–25 minutes until golden.
9 Serve warm or cold.
Makes about 16

As long as the earth endures, seedtime and harvest, cold and heat,
summer and winter, day and night will never cease.
Genesis 8:22 (NIV)

When I was a very little girl, I was quite shy of anything that happened to put me in the limelight (unlike now!). One Harvest Festival morning, I set off nervously down the aisle at church with my basket of fruit and eggs – and bumped into the child in front. One of the eggs cracked and, scarlet with shame, I fled back to my seat crying "Mummy, Mummy, I've ripped my egg!" What funny things we remember!

The days are largely gone now when churches could be seen bedecked with produce from farms, gardens and allotments and we distributed gifts of fruit and vegetables to the elderly or sick children in hospital. Last year, our church had a nominal harvest display and, instead, we made up boxes of staple foods such as flour, pasta and tinned fruit for needy families in Eastern Europe.

Even though few of us 'plough the fields and scatter' nowadays, it is good to continue the tradition of saying thank you to God for his faithfulness in keeping the world turning, and the seasons following each other, for our provision.

Human foolishness and greed are causing huge climate changes and destroying many resources, and we need to take urgent notice of the warning signs as we pollute the earth. But God is definitely still in charge.

A local preacher I have heard many times always praises the 'Creator of the rolling spheres and Potentate of time' in his prayers, using the reassuring words of an old hymn. These Harvest Pinwheels remind us of the Circle of Life which has no beginning and no end. It is good to remember that God lives outside of time and holds us in the palm of his hand during every season of the year.

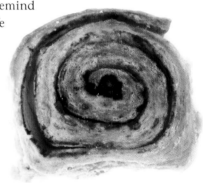

Summer and winter, and springtime and harvest,
Sun, moon and stars in their courses above,
Join with all nature in manifold witness
To thy great faithfulness, mercy and love.

(From *Great is thy Faithfulness*, Thomas O. Chisholm, 1866–1960)

Thank you, Father God, creator of all good things,
that you keep this world rolling on within your eternal plan. Amen

43

Honor's Apple and Sage Preserve

Honor, who tested and baked many of the recipes for this book, makes all kinds of wonderful preserves. This one is delicious with roast pork or cold meat. The lovely colour makes it an attractive gift – perhaps as part of a Christmas Hamper – or a jar would look good in a Harvest display.

Ingredients

900g (2lbs) cooking apples (windfalls are fine)
  or crab apples
A good bunch of fresh sage (washed)
Water
Sugar
A few washed and dried sage leaves,
  finely chopped (optional)

Method

1 Wash and cut up the apples including the whole fruit, skins and pips. If using windfalls, wash and make sure all bruises and blemishes are removed.

2 Put fruit into a large saucepan with the bunch of sage and cover with water.

3 Gently simmer until apple is pulped and broken down.

4 Strain through a muslin cloth. This can be tied to the four legs of an upturned kitchen stool with a large bowl underneath the cloth to catch the juice. Alternatively, use a purpose-made jelly strainer set which includes a bag and stand, available from good kitchen shops or from Lakeland Ltd. (www.lakeland.co.uk).

5 Allow to drip overnight – do not be tempted to squeeze bag as this will make the final jelly cloudy.

6 Next day measure juice and allow 450g (1lb) of sugar to each pint of juice.

7 Put measured juice into large saucepan or preferably a *maslin* pan and heat gently, adding sugar and stirring continuously until dissolved. Bring to boil, then boil rapidly until setting point is reached.

8 Skim off the scum and stir in dried, chopped sage, if liked.

9 Pot into warm, sterile jars and, when cool, label and store in cool dark place.

> My son, preserve sound judgment and discernment, do not let them out of your sight…
> Proverbs 3:21 (NIV)

Just before Christmas, some boys in one of our local supermarkets were offering to pack bags for customers. They had large colourful buckets at their sides with no obligation to pay but, if you wanted to make a small contribution, it would help towards providing a new sports' venue for young people.

It didn't matter (too much!) that, when we got home, we found the soap in with the bread nor that a bag of frozen vegetables had made the front pages of the newspaper unreadable. What mattered was the sense of camaraderie and cheerfulness amongst those young people and the knowledge that they were doing something for others which would also help create a much-needed community facility. This seemed such an antidote to the depressing tales of how many ASBOs local teenagers are collecting, that I paid up happily and went home smiling.

It's a sign of our times that Citizenship has to be taught as a separate subject in schools rather than simply being imbibed from good general, moral teaching and from adequate role models in society. A journalist on the radio this morning commented that there seems to be a swing back to moral teachings recently, in reaction to the way our national values are being watered down by so-called political correctness. Let's pray that it's true!

It's all about *preservation*. The laws of the land are based on the Ten Commandments but it's not just about keeping the law. It's about the mind-set of wanting to do the right thing for the benefit of society.

Oh, I know those boys would probably just have laughed at such a worthy motive but, nevertheless, they encouraged me. And if the bread tasted a bit soapy – well, it just reminded us that allowing others as well as ourselves to learn from mistakes is healthy when it is done in an atmosphere of loving acceptance.

Sage Jelly
25 November 20

Lord, sometimes the standards we value seem to be disappearing fast. Help us to preserve the good things that are happening in our communities and the world around us, and to be encouraged – and encouraging. Amen

Coffee Time Cookies

These crisp sophisticated biscuits which are very simple to make,
go down well with morning coffee. They could also be attractively wrapped
with some Fair Trade coffee or tea as a thoughtful gift.

Ingredients

225g (8oz) margarine
110g (4oz) caster sugar
1 medium egg
1 teaspoon vanilla essence
1 heaped tablespoon coffee granules
250g (9oz) self-raising flour
Demerara sugar to sprinkle

Method

1 Preheat oven to gas mark 4/180°C/350°F. Lightly grease two or more baking sheets.

2 Cream margarine and sugar together until light and fluffy.

3 Beat in egg and vanilla essence with a little sifted flour to prevent curdling.

4 Stir in coffee granules.

5 Fold in remaining flour.

6 Place rounded teaspoonfuls of the mixture on to the baking sheets, allowing room to spread. Alternatively use a nylon piping bag and large star nozzle, to pipe stars onto the baking sheets. Sprinkle with Demerara sugar. You might need to bake the cookies in two batches depending on the size of your oven.

7 Bake for about 12–15 minutes until golden. Cool on a wire rack.

Makes approximately 36 cookies

Be inventive in hospitality.

Romans 12:13 (The Message)

'Come round for a coffee.'
'Let's meet in town for a coffee.'
'We're having a Coffee Morning.'

What is it about coffee that gives an immediate warm, comfortable feeling? The fridge magnet that asks *Is there life before coffee?* may be overstating the case, but we get the point!

For a new friend or neighbour, an invitation to coffee is an informal way of showing hospitality and usually has a specific time-slot so it's easy to manage. Coffee Mornings, as well as being good fundraisers, are also an easy way to include newcomers in church activities. Whether its morning coffee or teatime, Sunday lunch or an evening meal, providing nourishment for the body is always a winner in friendship evangelism.

A church I heard of has set up a monthly Coffee House in their hall with small tables covered in bright fabric and a candle on each one to give a warm, inviting ambience. Live, and not necessarily Christian, music is played and interesting food is provided on different themes to match the time of year or special interests. The organisers aim to provide 'a wholesome family setting to help sow the seeds of God's love' to people who might find a church service uncomfortable, and it is thriving.

Did Mary and Martha hold Coffee Mornings? Well, as far as I know, coffee hadn't yet reached Palestine, but I'm pretty sure there was an equivalent as so many of Jesus' stories centre around food. The first miracle he performed was at a wedding party, turning water into wine to help out the host, and everyone knows the story of the loaves and fishes. The ultimate example is perhaps the Last Supper when he used the bread and wine as symbols of his body and blood. He knew that food was something everyone needed and to which everyone could relate.

So why not make a few goodies to show how much you care? Then, get the coffee pot out and be creative in who you invite to share coffee time with you!

PS It is said that goats actually discovered the coffee plant. Their shepherd noticed that they were getting very hyper; so, one day, he followed their every move and found out that they were eating a strange berry that was keeping them awake all day and night!

Lord, we want to share the good things of life with the people around us. Help us not only to 'wake up and smell the coffee' but to put the coffee pot on for everyone to share. Amen

Lights to the World

These lanterns, made from recycled glass, are ideal to brighten up your 'Light and Bright' alternative Halloween event. Place them on tables or shelves out of reach of younger guests, or in front of mirrors for double the effect – they could be used again for a candlelit carol service.

For a simpler idea that young children would enjoy, replace the glass painting with torn brightly-coloured tissue scraps pasted onto the outside of the jar. For safety, do not use any tissue paper around the neck of the jar. Alternatively, cut a double-thickness band of kitchen foil to fit round the circumference of the jar, cut and punch a pattern of holes in it and glue on securely. *Caution! Always supervise children around lighted candles.*

Ingredients

Jam or coffee jars, washed and dried
Gold glass painting outliner and red, orange and yellow glass paints
Ribbon or strips of coloured paper for neck of jar
Nightlights or other small candles
Blu Tack, clean sand or rice
Taper

Method

1 Rest jar on its side on an old folded towel or thick wedge of newspaper.
2 Either freehand or using templates cut from old cards or wrapping paper, draw outlines of stars, a moon, a candle or random patterns on one side of the jar using glass painting outliner. Allow to dry. Repeat on the opposite side and allow to dry. (Repeat on the remaining sides if you wish.)
3 Fill in shapes with coloured glass paints, allowing each side to dry in turn.
4 Glue ribbon or other trim round neck of jar, taking care to keep all decorations on the outside of the jar and away from the flame.
5 Either anchor a nightlight with *Blu Tack* or set a small, chunky candle in sand or rice in the bottom of the jar.
6 Use a taper to light the candle.

...God said, 'Light up the darkness!' and our lives filled up with light
as we saw and understood God in the face of Christ, all bright and beautiful.

2 Corinthians 4:6 (The Message)

I stood in the newsagents' queue gazing at hideous masks, Dracula fangs and witches' potions and just wanting Halloween to be over for another year. Still, it's only a bit of fun to brighten up the autumn, isn't it? Well, maybe it used to be....although I'm not even sure about that today...

I remember having a Halloween party as a teenager even though both my parents were church deacons. In those days, few people ever stopped to think about the true meaning of Halloween. In the 1960s, witches and spooks were simply an extension of the fairytales of childhood and we hardly ever heard anything about Satanism, Black Masses and the occult in general. Nowadays, the huge commercial emphasis placed on Halloween has encouraged Christians to consider where they stand on this issue.

Even if you don't believe that real forces of evil are at work around this season, the promotion of darkness over light and the anti-social practice of 'trick or treating' is not a wholesome experience for our vulnerable children. They live in a society that has already stripped them of their innocence too young. And I don't know too many elderly folk who relish answering the door to gruesome ghouls in horrible masks either.

So, rather than descend into gloom, why not hold a 'Light and Bright Party' instead? Many non-church parents would welcome an attractive, safe alternative for October 31 and it could be a powerful outreach tool. There are some excellent resources on the Christian bookshelves to get you started. You could encourage the wearing of bright glittery clothes, provide colourful food – perhaps Make-Your-Own Pizza with a variety of bright ingredients? And play some of the traditional games such as apple-bobbing, doughnut-dangling, parachute games or a scavenger hunt.

Most of all, let's show children that they can have the courage to face all the dark things of this world that they will inevitably meet, if they claim the promise of the light of Jesus' love.

Lord, we live in a world where many people prefer to creep around under cover of darkness because they are afraid of the challenge of the light. Help us to shine the light of your love into the darkest corners. Amen

Starlight Cookies

Serve these delightful cookies at your 'Light and Bright Party',
or make them with a hole through one point to hang on the Christmas tree!
Either way they are delicious biscuits which will be popular with all ages.

Ingredients

200g (7oz) plain flour
110g (4oz) butter
75g (3oz) caster sugar
1 medium egg, beaten
110g (4oz) icing sugar
1 lemon

Method

1 Preheat oven to gas mark 6/200°C/400°F. Lightly grease two baking sheets.
2 Sift flour into a large bowl and rub in the butter.
3 Add the sugar and beaten egg, then mix to a smooth dough.
4 Roll out to approximately ½cm (¼in) thickness and cut into stars with a cutter.
5 Place carefully on baking tray and, if using to hang on the tree, make a hole in one point of star with a skewer.
6 Bake for about 12 minutes until golden, then cool on a wire rack.
7 When cold, mix sieved icing sugar with a teaspoon of finely grated lemon zest and enough lemon juice to make an icing thin enough to drizzle over the cookies. Allow to set for several hours.
8 If using as tree decorations, thread each cookie with narrow ribbon.
Makes dozens of cookies!

When our church's young people returned from their annual camp, we could tell from their glowing faces that something special had happened even before they told us. Then, one after the other, they stood up in the morning service to recount a deeply emotional time of worship and sharing out under the stars, during which God had touched each of their hearts in an incredibly powerful way. There were not many dry eyes among the rest of us that morning.

Later, one of the leaders told me that a young lad who had lost his voice through too much shouting and whooping during games, whispered a prayer that had touched everyone from the oldest to the youngest.

The Psalmist, gazing up at that same night sky, had been almost overwhelmed by the vastness and power of God's creation, but he recognised that humankind was even more wonderful as he wrote: *You made him a little lower than the heavenly beings and crowned him with glory and honour.* (Psalm 8:4)

It is difficult to grasp the fact that the light from some of the stars we can see has taken millions of years to reach us, isn't it? But that scientific fact helps me to appreciate the magnitude of creation and to feel amazed and awed that I have a part to play in eternity.

The Book of Daniel says: *Those who are wise will shine like the brightness of the heavens, and those who lead many to righteousness, like the stars for ever and ever.* (Daniel 12:3)

As I listened to, and watched, 'cool' young people shining with a brightness that only the Lord could have lit, I was hugely encouraged. Far from the truth of the gospel being lost to the next generation, there will always be a core of people who will recognise God's hand in creation and listen to his voice inspiring them to follow him and make disciples of others.

Lord, thank you that you continue to reveal yourself to each generation. May we, young and old, be stars for you, leading others to know your love and power in their lives. Amen

Bonfire Cake

A Bonfire Party can be a great event to involve people on the fringe of the church. Serve the cake with sparklers stuck in the top and lit by an adult for a fiery impact!

This cake also works well with a chocolate and orange sponge mixture. You could also make the gingerbread in a loaf tin for other occasions.

Ingredients

2 medium eggs
110g (4oz) soft brown sugar
4 rounded tablespoons black treacle
250ml (10fl oz) very hot water
110g (4oz) margarine
110g (4oz) crystallised ginger, chopped
350g (12oz) plain flour
2 teaspoons bicarbonate of soda
2 heaped teaspoons
    ground ginger

For icing

Apricot jam (optional)
75g (3oz) soft margarine
175g (6oz) icing sugar
50g (2oz) drinking
    chocolate powder
A scant tablespoon
    of milk
Chocolate matchsticks
    (orange or
    honeycomb flavour)
Dolly mixture and
    other flame-coloured
    sweets

Method

1 Preheat oven to gas mark 5/190°C/375°F. Grease a 1 litre (2 pint) pudding basin and cut a circle of greaseproof to line the bottom.
2 In a large bowl, beat the egg with the sugar and treacle.
3 Put hot water in a jug and melt margarine in it. Then stir in crystallised ginger and pour onto egg mixture, stirring well.
4 Sift flour, bicarbonate of soda and ground ginger together; stir into mixture until well combined.
5 Pour into greased pudding basin and bake for about 40 minutes until a fine skewer inserted in the middle comes out clean.
6 Cool on a wire rack, then slice horizontally into three layers and spread with apricot jam, if desired. Reassemble on a board or plate.
7 Beat the margarine, sieved icing sugar and drinking chocolate together with enough milk to make a spreading consistency.
8 Cover cake with icing, arrange chocolate matchsticks to represent firewood and intersperse with sweets to represent fireworks and flames.

By day the Lord went ahead of them in a pillar of cloud to guide them
on their way and by night in a pillar of fire to give them light...

Exodus 13:21 (NIV)

I love the smell of wood-smoke on a crisp autumn afternoon. Bonfire Night conjures up happy memories of my Dad and brother building up a big fire in our garden, while Mum and I prepared food for the friends and neighbours who would join us. Hot soup and jacket potatoes with lashings of butter, cheese and home-made chutney...mmm...

Fire is often used in the Bible to represent God's presence and his power. Fire symbolises a warming, creative force, which can also be highly dangerous if misused.

The story of Shadrach, Meshach and Abednego in the fiery furnace used to be one of my favourites as a child. The appearance of God's protecting angel in the flames thrilled me. Then, as I grew up, I gradually realised that whatever 'fire' I had to walk through in life, God would be there beside me.

Sometimes we have to go through very hard times in order for the Lord to change us for the better. As a modern translation of God's words spoken through the prophet Isaiah puts it: *Do you see what I've done? I've refined you, but not without fire. I've tested you in the furnace of affliction.* (Isaiah 48:10 The Message) However hard it is at the time, we can often look back and be glad of God's refining hand in our lives.

And as we reach out to others, let's stop and take note of something the famous preacher C.H. Spurgeon said: "You must go into the fire if you are going to pull others out of it."

Next time you are near a real fire, gaze at it for a moment and wonder at the power and the warmth that the fire of God's love creates.

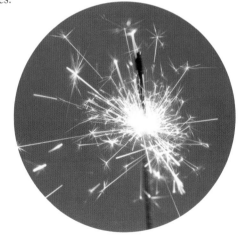

Lord of light and warmth, send the fire that will burn away all the rubbish
in my life and leave me a cleaner, better person. Amen

Nuggets of Gold

Small savoury biscuits are a favourite of mine and this is a particularly scrummy recipe.
I have sometimes given them to friends going on a self-catering holiday to enjoy
with a glass of wine in the evening.

Ingredients

110g (4oz) plain white flour
50g (2oz) plain wholemeal flour
1 level teaspoon mustard powder
1 level teaspoon paprika
Pinch of salt
75g (3oz) butter
75g (3oz) strong cheddar cheese,
  finely grated
Small onion, finely chopped and softened
  in a little oil (optional)
Freshly-grated parmesan and/or Red
  Leicester cheese for sprinkling
  (optional)

Method

1 Preheat oven to gas mark 5/190°C/375°F. Lightly grease
  a baking sheet.
2 Sift flours into a bowl with the other dry ingredients
  and tip in any bran left in the sieve.
3 Rub in butter until mixture resembles fine
  breadcrumbs. Stir in grated cheddar cheese and onion.
4 Break off walnut-sized pieces of the mixture and roll
  into balls.
5 Place on baking sheet and slightly
  flatten each nugget with a fork.
  Sprinkle with parmesan and/or
  Red Leicester, if using, to add colour
  and flavour.
6 Bake in centre of oven for 15-20
  minutes or until golden. Turn tray
  halfway through baking.
7 Cool on a wire rack. Store in an
  airtight box in the fridge.
  Makes about 18

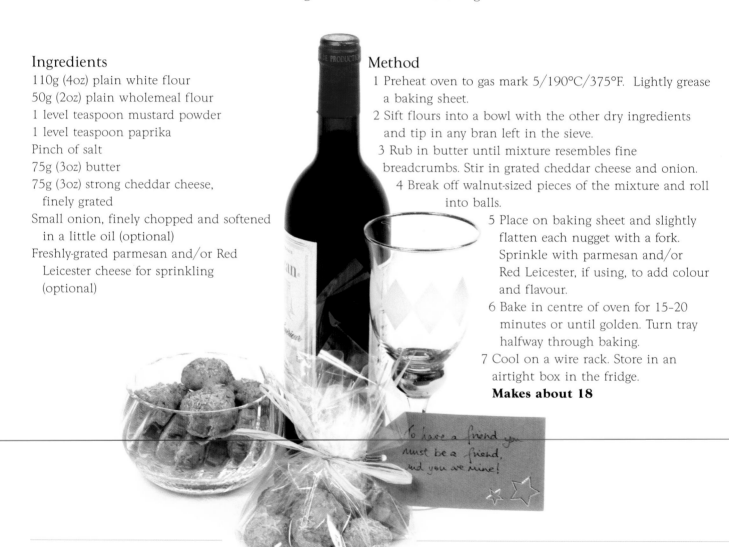

To have a friend you
must be a friend,
and you are mine!

For an unusual gift, pack up a portion of the biscuits in a generous piece of cellophane and tie on a gift tag with one or more of the following 'Golden Nuggets' of wisdom written on it.

Happiness is a wonderful thing –
the more you give,
the more you have.

Turn your face towards the sun
and the shadows will fall behind you.
(From a sundial in Carnoustie, Scotland.)

Spread your wings – seek the farthest reaches
of your world.

Give God your heart, your service and your gold.
The day wears on and time is waxing old.
(From a sundial at Gloucester Cathedral.)

More things are wrought by prayer
than this world dreams of. (Tennyson)

It is better to light just one candle
than to curse the darkness.

What you are is God's gift to you
What you make of yourself is your gift to God.

Pray for sunshine – and
be prepared to be
part of God's
answer!

A friend is
someone who
knows all about
you and loves
you just the same.

The value of life
lies not in the length of
our days but in the use we
make of them.

To have a friend you must be a friend, and you
are mine!

Treasure yesterday, dream tomorrow, live today.

P.S. A nugget of gold given at the right time can truly bless a friend, but there might be the odd time when it's better to keep quiet! Consider this quote while you decide...

Wisdom has two parts:
1) Having a lot to say. 2) Not saying it.

Lord, help me to be an encourager; to know when to speak and when to be silent, but always to bring your love into every situation I meet. Amen

55

Bowls of Gratitude

This is a simple way of saying a special thank you to someone who has helped you in some way this year. You will need to plant the bulbs in good time for them to flower around Christmas.

You will need:

Pottery bowl - buy new or recycle old one
Potting compost
Hyacinth, crocus or narcissi bulbs
Lollipop stick or similar
Gift card

Instructions

1 Make sure bowl is clean and dry. Plant bulbs in potting compost following supplier's instructions.
2 When ready to give, arrange gift wrap or coloured tissue loosely around the bowl or simply add a bow.
3 Add a gift card with a suitable greeting such as, *Thank you for your friendship...it means a lot!* An easy card can be made by sticking a picture of the appropriate flower from a gardening catalogue, or the header card from your pack of bulbs, onto thin card and attaching it to a lollipop stick.
4 You might like to add the words of a suitable Bible verse, in which case one of the following might be appropriate:

I always thank God for you because of his grace given you in Christ Jesus. (1 Corinthians 1:4)

I have not stopped giving thanks for you, remembering you in my prayers. (Ephesians 1:16)

The LORD bless you and keep you; the LORD make his face shine upon you and be gracious to you; the LORD turn his face toward you and give you peace. (Numbers 6:24-26)

The grace of the Lord Jesus be with you. (1 Corinthians 16:24)

May the God of hope fill you with all joy and peace as you trust in him, so that you may overflow with hope by the power of the Holy Spirit. (Romans 15:13)

It was a family tradition when I was a little girl that we went to Rugby on the Saturday before Christmas for last-minute present shopping.

Outside an old-fashioned ironmonger's shop my Dad rested one knee on a stone bird bath in order to look more closely at something in the window. I was always wanting to copy him so I tried this when he moved away – and the bird bath toppled and broke.

I was distraught as Dad hauled me into the shop to apologise. But, instead of accepting Dad's offered payment for the damaged goods, the shopkeeper gave me a bowl of hyacinths because he felt so sorry for me. Ever since, each time I smell the distinctive scent of those flowers, that lovely man's compassion floods over me again and they have remained one of my very favourites. He's probably long-since gone, but if anyone in Rugby remembers an ironmonger with a kind heart, I'd love to hear from them!

That incident has been a little parable for me of the way in which God forgives us for our mistakes and loves us unconditionally. The saying *A friend is someone who knows all about you and loves you just the same* often heartens me when I've said or done something stupid in company. I have some lovely friends who forgive me much!

I have just read in my daily Bible notes: *Nothing goes unnoticed by God, and every act of kindness and love – however small – is an act of worship that he values.* Any gift can express our love and gratitude to someone, but a present we have put some personal effort into is extra special.

Thank you, Lord, for the acts of kindness that brighten our days.
Show us ways we can pass the kindness on and spread blessings to those around us. Amen

Bird Pudding

Don't try eating this yourself! This pudding would make a great gift for the birds in your garden – or give it to a house-bound friend who enjoys bird-watching. It is an excellent way to use up stale cake and biscuit scraps while providing some extra fat to keep birds warm in winter.

The string is optional as the pudding can simply be placed on the bird table. However, if you hang it from a tree, it will attract the smaller birds such as blue tits and chaffinches.

Ingredients
Lard, suet or dripping
Stale cake and/or biscuits
Any out-of-date baking ingredients
such as raisins, dates,
nuts etc
Table scraps

Method
1 Melt fat in a saucepan.
2 Add crumbled cake or biscuits, chopped up baking ingredients and table scraps. Mix well.
3 Knot a piece of string about 30cm (12in) long and place knot down in a small pudding basin or carton lined with cling film.
4 Press mixture into basin around string, leaving its end over the side.
5 Refrigerate until set, then hang in the garden.

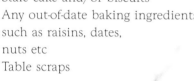

I was making a jelly, when a drama on the lawn caught my eye.

There was a squabble going on over a few scraps of pitta bread from the bird table. The starlings, like naughty boys, were jostling each other while a hen blackbird – Primary School Head – repeatedly told them off and shooed them away. A few cheeky sparrows joined in and a plump pigeon, reminding me of a short-sighted maiden aunt, bumbled around ignored by all.

Suddenly a hooded crow swooped down from nowhere and, in panic, they all scattered. He picked up the largest piece of bread and disappeared. Back they all flocked.

The hen blackbird's authority was challenged by a thrush who seemed quite angry about the whole affair. Then the blackbird's mate made an appearance and the starlings flew to the treetops to watch and wait – all except one youth on gangly legs who continued to peck around for crumbs. The hen blackbird stopped what she was doing and cocked her head on one side, evidently amazed at his nerve.

Then my husband pointed out the time and I had to fly off (well, you know what I mean!) to keep an appointment.

That little scene in the garden had kept me spellbound as it seemed so *human*. I now understood the origin of the term 'pecking order'! In the end, no bird had gone without, but each had different needs and different ways of addressing them.

Are we resolved to get along with our fellow humans, simply taking what we need but leaving enough for others? Are we prepared to share God's resources? Above all, do we trust God – who even cares about little sparrows or canaries, sold two for a penny – to provide for our every need?

An Advent Snowman

When I was little, my Great-Grandma had a Crinoline Doll, hiding tiny wrapped presents under her skirt, which absolutely enthralled me! The snowman in the picture was a variation made for a Snowman Festival and I based it on a jar of chocolates. Later, the children in our choir had great fun cascading them into a basket to share.

Ingredients

A large empty plastic sweet jar (beg from a shop)
Craft knife
Masking tape
White fabric (an old sheet or towel is ideal)
Newspaper
Cotton wool
Black and coloured card
Fabric adhesive (*Copydex*)
Cakeboard or piece of cardboard
Assortment of 24 tiny wrapped gifts, sweets or ideas for activities

Method

1 Remove lid from jar. Using a craft knife, carefully cut a rounded door shape out of one side. (Bind with masking tape if the edges seem rough.)
2 Cut a rough circle of white fabric large enough to drape over the sweet jar for the body and another large enough to cover a ball of newspaper for the head.
3 Wrap the ball of newspaper in the fabric and pass the loose ends through a slit in the fabric across the neck of the jar. Secure inside with tape if necessary.
4 Make a top hat from the black card. Cut features such as a carrot nose and coal eyes from coloured card and stick on. Add cut-out gloves.
5 If you have time, knit a stripy scarf to wind round the neck. Otherwise, make it from coloured paper or fabric.
6 Stand the snowman on a cake board or cardboard cut from a carton and painted. Place the little gifts in the 'door' of the snowman under the loose fabric.
7 Each day during Advent, family members take turns at drawing out one of the gifts or ideas from the snowman. Alternatively, fill the snowman with tiny gifts for a Sunday School party or similar.

The weeks leading up to Christmas are often frantic times of hustle and bustle as we shop, bake and attend school and church Nativity plays and concerts. The word 'Advent' means the coming or arrival of Jesus and it is good to remember that his birth was foretold hundreds of years before, in Old Testament times.

Advent calendars, which mark the passing of time up to Christmas Day, were first produced in Germany in the late 19th century. Sadly, however, they have now become so commercialised that many have lost their Christian significance and are often only an excuse for children to indulge in chocolate. Hiding some activities, such as quizzes or word-searches based on the Nativity story, in your snowman can be a way of redressing the balance. Or perhaps make an Advent Angel holding a Carol Sheet instead... Oh, the ideas are flowing now!

A Snowman Festival in church during Advent could be a good outreach event. Invite local schools, Brownies, Flower Guilds and other organisations to enter a snowman, and provide refreshments, competitions and publicity about your Christmas services for visitors who might otherwise never come to church.

As we wait for Christmas Day, it's good to remind ourselves of the three aspects of the 'coming' of Jesus.

First, he came as a vulnerable human baby at a specific time in history to show a hurting world that God understood and identified with its plight.

Secondly, he came as a Saviour who loved the world so much that he was prepared to die for it and cancel out all the sin that had been, or would be, committed, giving a second chance to all who believed in him.

But thirdly, he is coming again! The writer of the book of Revelation foresees this amazing truth: *Look, he is coming with the clouds, and every eye will see him, even those who pierced him, and all the peoples of the earth will mourn because of him. So shall it be, Amen. I am the Alpha and the Omega, says the Lord God, who is and who was and who is to come, the Almighty.* (Revelation 1:7–8)

Amongst all the razzmatazz of Christmas, let's spend some time ourselves preparing our hearts and minds for that glorious day.

Lord of the past, the present and the future, we worship and adore you and look forward to the time when we will see you face-to-face. Amen

61

Christmas Kisses

Give these away in a pretty container or keep at hand for visitors
over the festive season. They originate from Scandinavia where it is believed
that a visitor who leaves without being fed may carry the Christmas spirit away!

Ingredients

110g (4oz) butter
50g (2oz) caster sugar
1 large egg yolk.
175g (6oz) plain flour
1 level teaspoon ground cinnamon
Icing sugar to dust

Method

1 Preheat oven to gas mark 6/200°C/400°F. Lightly grease
  2 baking sheets.
2 Cream butter and sugar until light and fluffy.
3 Beat in egg yolk.
4 Stir in flour and cinnamon to give a dry-ish mixture.
  (If the mixture is too dry to work easily, add 1 teaspoon
  of milk.)
5 Take walnut sized pieces of the dough and roll into long
  fingers about 14cm (5½in) in length. Place on baking
  sheets crossing over to make kisses. Cut the loop at the
  top to make kiss shapes or leave intact to make icthus
  fishes (see picture right).
6 Bake for 10–12 minutes until golden.
7 Remove carefully and place on a wire rack to cool.
8 Dust with icing sugar.
  Makes approximately 24

Greet one another with a kiss of love. Peace to all of you who are in Christ.

1 Peter 5:14 (NIV)

It was the middle of summer and the congregation of the Free Church where I worshipped was not used to exchanging *The Peace* like our Anglican friends. I went up to a dear old man who always had a cheery word when he gave out the hymnbooks.

"The Peace of the Lord be with you," I said solemnly, shaking his hand.

"Happy Christmas!" he chirruped back, missing the point entirely, but planting a smacker of a kiss soundly on my lips. Not quite what the minister had in mind, but I felt very loved!

I heard of another church where the congregation was growing in size as love was expressed not only in words and deeds but also in uninhibited hugs and kisses. Then suddenly it all stopped – and just because someone was afraid it would get out of hand or be misinterpreted in this age of political correctness.

We shouldn't be afraid to put an arm round a grieving friend either; just a squeeze of a hand can sometimes say more than a thousand words. When Gladys, an elderly lady in my Home Group, was widowed she said tearfully "It's the cuddles I miss most." Fortunately, she had children and grandchildren who could help to fill the gap but there are many single people whose only physical contact in a week may be a handshake at arm's length.

During the Party Season it may be easier to express affection, but let's make it Christmas every day as we share the Godly hugs I'm sure he wants us to pass on!

Lord, you were not afraid to touch the man with leprosy, to take the hand of Jairus's little daughter or to anoint the eyes of the blind man. Help us to use the gift of touch in a wholesome way to express your love to someone today. Amen

Lollipops from the Tree

My friend Kathleen introduced me to the idea of choosing small inexpensive Tree
Gifts for friends and relatives for whom we perhaps don't buy a bigger present.
These Lollipop Cookies can be enjoyed by unexpected adult visitors as well as children!

Ingredients

110g (4oz) butter
75g (3oz) granulated sugar
Yolk of one medium egg
150g (5oz) plain flour
175g (6oz) multi-coloured glacé cherries, chopped
12 flat wooden lollipop sticks

Method

1 Preheat oven to gas mark 5/190°C/375°F and grease
  2 baking sheets.
2 Cream butter and sugar until light and fluffy, then beat in
  egg yolk.
3 Stir in flour and half of cherries. Mix to a firm dough.
4 Divide the dough into 12 small balls and place 6 on each
  baking sheet.
5 Flatten slightly and push a lollipop stick about halfway into
  each ball. Press on remaining cherries.
6 Bake for approximately 15 minutes. Cool on wire rack.
7 When cold, wrap individually in cellophane and tie on tree
  with ribbon.
Makes 12 lollipop cookies

> To him who overcomes, I will give the right to eat from the tree of life, which is in the paradise of God.
>
> Revelation 2:7 (NIV)

Trees are a theme throughout the Bible, from the fall of Adam and Eve by eating forbidden fruit in Genesis to the promise of reconciliation with God in Revelation. And when Peter spoke to the Gentiles in Caesarea he described Jesus' death as hanging on a tree (Acts 10:39).

Trees are essential for so many reasons – to give shade and protection, to provide timber, fruit and fuel and as homes for animals and birds – not to mention the beauty that they add to our countryside and gardens. A landscape without trees can seem very barren indeed.

A delightful legend tells us how the Holy Family hid from Herod's soldiers in a clump of cedar trees when they were fleeing to Egypt. The trees, which used to lose their leaves every winter like other trees, grew green needles in order to shield the family, with their white berries turning blue to disguise Mary's robe so that the whole family could escape unnoticed. From then on, the cedar was an evergreen.

In the Middle Ages, an evergreen tree was decorated with apples and bread to symbolise the Tree of the Knowledge of Good and Evil and the Tree of Life. It was known as the Paradise Tree and was used in Medieval Mystery Plays.

When they were first brought indoors to decorate the house, trees were hung upside down. Martin Luther introduced lights in the form of candles onto the tree after he had seen stars twinkling through the branches of evergreens. And, of course, the Christmas tree as we now know it was introduced to Britain from Germany by Prince Albert in the 19th century.

Hanging special gifts from the focal point of our Christmas decorations can be a reminder of the greatest gift of all, our Lord and Saviour Jesus Christ.

This Christmas-time, Lord, give us a fresh sense of your presence
as we give and receive gifts to celebrate your birthday. Amen

The Legend of the Poinsettia

This delightful Christmas legend is worth sharing with friends.
Why not accompany the story with either a real plant or this unusual Christmas log?

Ingredients

3 medium eggs
75g (3oz) caster sugar
½ teaspoon vanilla essence
75g (3oz) self-raising flour
Icing sugar to dredge

Filling:
284ml (10fl oz) double cream, whipped
Strawberry or seedless raspberry jam

Icing:
200g (7oz) plain chocolate
2 teaspoons of butter
2-3 tablespoons of hot water

Method

1 Preheat oven to gas mark 7/220°C/425°F. Grease and line a 23cm x 30cm (9in x12in) Swiss roll tin. Brush the greaseproof paper lightly with oil or melted, unsalted butter.
2 Whisk eggs, sugar and vanilla essence together with an electric whisk until double the size, very light in colour and the texture of softly-whipped cream. This will take three or four minutes (it helps to warm the bowl before you start).
3 Sieve the flour into the bowl and fold in very gently.
4 Pour mixture into lined tin and spread evenly into corners.
5 Bake near top of oven for 8–10 minutes until golden and the centre springs back when touched.
6 Roll out a large sheet of greaseproof paper and dredge with icing sugar. Turn sponge out, upside down, onto paper. Peel away lining paper from sponge and trim any uneven edges.
7 Roll up the hot sponge from a short end with the paper inside and leave to cool.
8 Whip cream until it forms soft peaks.
9 Carefully unroll the sponge and discard paper. Spread with jam and cream and then roll up again, holding in position for a minute. Keep the open edge at the bottom to ensure the cake can't unroll!
10 Ice with melted plain chocolate, mixed with butter and hot water. Use a fork to give a log-like texture.
11 Dredge with icing sugar to look like snow.
12 Make poinsettia flowers out of coloured marzipan. If you enjoy sugar craft, use a calyx cutter, or cut round a small leaf and join five leaves in a star shape. To create the appearance of leaf veins, press a washed, dry leaf onto the marzipan.

For if the willingness is there, the gift is acceptable according to what one has,
not according to what he does not have.

2 Corinthians 8:12 (NIV)

The poinsettia, a plant that brightens up the dark winter months, originates in Mexico. Possibly because of its starry shape and the rich red colour that reminds us of the sacrifice of Jesus, it was used by Franciscan monks in the 17th century in their processions. It was then introduced to the USA in the 19th century by Joel Poinsett, a skilled botanist, and has now become a very familiar part of our Christmas scene.

The Mexican legend associated with the poinsettia is a lovely illustration of giving from the heart.

A young girl wanted to take a gift to the Christmas crib in her village church but was too poor to buy anything. Her cousin assured her that the Christ child would accept any humble gift as long as it was given with love, so the girl went and gathered weeds from the roadside and arranged them into a bouquet as best she could.

As the girl laid her simple gift on the altar, she felt her spirit lift and suddenly the weeds were transformed into the most beautiful flaming red flowers shaped like the Christmas star. The villagers knew they had witnessed a miracle and from that day on the blooms were known as 'Flowers of the Holy Night'. A simple story perhaps... but a reminder that God accepts the smallest thing we do for him and often transforms it into a miracle. Perhaps you could tell the story at a Christmas tea, or maybe write it out to give away with the cake or a real poinsettia plant. It would certainly make an unusual and thought-provoking gift.

What can I give him, poor as I am?
If I were a shepherd I would bring a lamb,
If I were a wise man I would do my part,
Yet what I can I give him – give my heart.

(From *In the Bleak Midwinter* by Christina Rossetti, 1830–94)

Lord, give me the opportunity to touch someone new
with the simplicity of your gospel this Christmas time. Amen

Epiphany Cake

This scrummy, moist and light celebration cake will make a change for jaded palates after Christmas. I used it instead of a traditional Christmas cake this year, but why not make Twelfth Night, January 6, a special date on your calendar as we remember that Jesus came for all mankind and not just his own people?

Ingredients

225g (8oz) butter
225g (8oz) caster sugar
50g (2oz) ground almonds
350g (12oz) self-raising flour
3 teaspoons mixed spice
1 teaspoon cinnamon
1 teaspoon nutmeg
4 medium eggs
425g (15oz) tin crushed pineapple in natural juice
225g (8oz) dried ready-to-eat apricots, chopped
175g (6oz) glacé cherries, chopped
50g (2oz) chopped peel
Apricot jam
1 x 454g (1lb) pack marzipan
1 x 454g (1lb) Pack ready-to-roll icing or royal icing

Method

1 Preheat oven to gas mark 2/160°C/300°F. Grease and line a 21cm (8½in) round, loose-bottomed cake tin with a double layer of greaseproof paper.
2 Cream butter and sugar together until light and fluffy, then stir in ground almonds.
3 Beat eggs together in a jug and add to mixture gradually with a little sieved flour to prevent curdling.
4 Add remaining flour and spices and fold into mixture.
5 Drain pineapple and fold into mixture with apricots, cherries and chopped peel. Add a little of juice if mixture seems dry. Spoon into prepared tin and level surface.
6 Cook in centre of oven for 2–2½ hours, covering with foil or greaseproof paper if it seems to be browning too quickly. Cake will be ready when a fine skewer inserted in middle comes out clean. Leave to cool for a few minutes, then turn out carefully and finish cooling on a wire rack.
7 When completely cold, brush top with sieved apricot jam. Cover top and sides with rolled marzipan.
8 Roll a circle of icing to fit the top and a strip to fit the sides of cake. Brush marzipan lightly with water and place icing over. Crimp edges between finger and thumb and trim off any excess. Alternatively, use royal icing.
9 Finish with a gold paper crown and tinsel, and add the three kings from your nativity set to the top of the cake; or mould three kings out of icing. The figures in our picture were made from half flower paste icing and half fondant icing blended together.

The names Caspar, Melchior and Balthazar were probably just an invention since they don't appear in the Bible, but I still get a tingle down my spine whenever we sing *We Three Kings* and different members of our choir take the solo verses.

The arrival of the rich strangers who followed a star to bring Jesus deeply meaningful gifts is a vital and exciting part of the story and deserves to have its own celebration. Epiphany means the 'manifesting' or 'showing' of Jesus to the non-Jewish Magi, emphasising that the gospel message was to be for everybody.

I like the custom of leaving the three kings out of the nativity scene when it is put up on Christmas Eve and helping them to 'travel' to the stable over the holiday period. They could start off at the top of the house, or at the back of the church, for instance, and gradually move towards the centrepiece each day, guided by a movable star!

Many countries have their own traditions about Epiphany, or Twelfth Night. One of the most poignant is the Russian story of Baboushka, whose name means 'little grandma'. This peasant woman gave hospitality to the three kings when they were on their way to see the new-born Jesus and they asked her to go with them. But she made excuses saying she was too busy and, when she changed her mind later and set off alone with toys for the baby, she couldn't find the way and to this day is still searching and leaving a toy wherever she finds a child.

Let's not leave it too late in *our* lives to find Jesus!

New Year Promise Crackers

For a simpler idea, place a promise in a prettily folded serviette at each place setting.

This is a fun way to add interest to your New Year's Day table.
You can use ready-made crackers or a make-your-own kit
if you want an easier version.

You will need:

Crepe paper
Thin card
Double-sided sticky tape
Coloured or metallic paper (wrapping paper is ideal)
Cracker snaps
Narrow gift ribbon
Printed promises, for example:

I promise to take you on a special mystery day out.
I promise to do your mending for a month.
I promise to cook and serve a dinner party at your house.
I promise to deliver two home-baked cakes next month.
I promise to babysit overnight on the date of your choice.
I promise to give you 3 hours gardening.....

Instructions

1 Cut a rectangle of crepe paper 45cm x 20cm (18in x 8in).
2 Cut 3 rectangles of thin card each 22cm x 10cm (9in x 4in).
  Roll each into a cylinder and secure with double-sided
  sticky tape.
3 Lay strips of double-sided tape across the crepe paper for
  attaching card cylinders, one across the middle, one at each
  end about 4cm (1½in) in. Position the cylinders, leaving gaps
  for tying ends.
4 Roll up and secure with double-sided tape.
5 Decorate with coloured paper bands and any other crafty
  bits to hand.
6 Insert cracker snap and promise.
7 Tie off ends with bows of gift ribbon.
8 To personalise the crackers, add a printed or hand-written
  name on top of each cracker.

This is exactly what Christ promised: eternal life, real life!

1 John 2:25 (The Message)

How often have you made a promise with the best of intentions and then broken it, simply because you forgot? When I have something essential to remember, I write it either in my diary or on the back of my hand where I can't miss it!

My New Year Promises, written down and given to other people, are different to Resolutions because I feel bound to keep them in all but the most extreme circumstances. So my friend Dorothy, who has mobility problems and no transport of her own, could look forward to a day trip in the car tailored to her needs. And we had a lovely time on a scorching day in July at Rutland Water.

Mum called in my promise of help with putting her paperwork in some sort of logical order very early in the year, but Ern reckons I didn't manage his ten hours of weeding the flower beds...Still, we are hoping to move to a bungalow with a low-maintenance garden so it's no longer relevant, and this year's promise is to create some magnificent tubs and hanging baskets instead!

God's promises to us are completely dependable and are contained in his Word. After the flood, he made a promise, or covenant, with Noah that the earth would never suffer such destruction again.

The Covenant Services, which some churches hold on the first Sunday of the year, give members of the congregation a chance to renew their promises to God and each other. Such a service also helps us to listen again to what God might want us to do next for him.

Although we *can't* exactly give the Unseen Guest a Promise Cracker at our New Year's Day lunch table, we *can* make our personal promises to the Lord as we begin a New Year – and resolve to keep them with his help.

Lord, every promise you make to us you keep.
Help me to make promises I genuinely can keep
and to be creative in making them to meet the needs of others. Amen

Useful addresses

The profits from the sale of this book go to support the work of
The Leprosy Mission in hospitals and rehabilitation workshops abroad.

TLM TRADING LIMITED
To buy books, gifts and craft items made by
leprosy affected people contact us at...
PO Box 212, Peterborough, PE2 5GD, UK
Tel: 0845 1662253   Fax: 01733 239258
Email: enquiries@tlmtrading.com
www.tlmtrading.com

TLM INTERNATIONAL
80 Windmill Road, Brentford,
Middlesex, TW8 0QH, UK.
Tel: 020 8326 6767   Fax: 020 8326 6777
Email: friends@tlmint.org
www.leprosymission.org

TLM ENGLAND AND WALES
www.leprosymission.org.uk

TLM NORTHERN IRELAND
www.tlm-ni.org

TLM SCOTLAND
www.tlmscotland.org.uk

The Leprosy Mission has offices all around the world.
Please contact TLM International if you would like contact details
for any of the following offices:

Africa Regional Office, Australia, Belgium, Canada, Denmark, Finland,
France, Germany, Hungary, India Regional Office, Ireland, Italy,
Netherlands, New Zealand, Portugal, South-East Asia Regional Office,
South Africa, Spain, Sweden, Switzerland, USA (Assoc Org), Zimbabwe